Faith Here and Now

Sermons Matter Series

Karen Russell

PARSON'S PORCH BOOKS

2018

Parson's Porch Books
www.parsonsporchbooks.com

Faith Here and Now
ISBN: Softcover 978-1-946478-74-0
Copyright © 2018 by Karen Russell

All rights reserved. No part of this book may be reproduced or transmitted in any form or by any means, electronic or mechanical, including photocopying, recording, or by any information storage and retrieval system, without permission in writing from the publisher.

Faith Here and Now

Contents

Introduction 9

Looking for a Sign 11
   Isaiah 7.10-16; Matthew 1.18-25

New Year, New Resolutions 15
   Matthew 2.13-23

The Order of the Law 19
   Matthew 5.21-37

There's a Light 24
   Isaiah 9.2-6; Luke 2.1-14

Bread, Bath, and Beyond 27
   Mark 1.4-11

Come and See 33
   1 Samuel 3.1-10; John 1.43-51

I Love a Parade 37
   Luke 19.28-40

From Palm Sunday to Good Friday 41
   Mark 1.1-11

When Worlds Collide 45
   John 3.1-2, 20-32

Breathe In, Breathe Out 49
   John 20.19-31

A Higher Law 54
   Acts 11.1-18; John 13.31-35

A Mighty Wind 59
   Acts 2.1-21

Freedom: Not Just Another Word 63
   Galatians 5.1, 13-25; Luke 9.51-62

Great Expectations 69
   Mark 6.1-13

Simplicity, Interrupted 74
   John 6.56-69

Strange Bedfellows 79
   Matthew 22.5-22

For All the Saints 83
   Isaiah 25.6-9; Revelation 21.1-6a

Jars of Clay 89
   1 Thessalonians 5.1-11

Metamorphosis 93
   Luke 9.28-36; 2 Corinthians 3.12-4.2

The Faith to Step Up 97
   Luke 7.1-10

Living Stones 101
   Acts 7.55-60; 1 Peter 2.1-10

The Message 105
   Luke 2.41-52

Faith: It's More than Wishin' and Hopin' 109
   Genesis 17.1-7, 15-16; Romans 4.13-25

Why Can't We All Just Get Along? 114
   Acts 4.32-33; Psalm 133
If There Be Any Encouragement.. 118
   Philippians 2.1-13
Love Is All You Need... 122
   Romans 13.8-14; Matthew 18.15-20
Pay Attention! 127
   Exodus 3.1-5
Faith Here and Now 131
   Hebrews 11.1-16; Luke 12.32-40
Re-Focusing... 135
   Luke 10.38-42
Kum Bah Ya... 141
   Ephesians 4.25-5.2; John 6.35,41-51
Sowing and Reaping–An Exercise in Hope 146
   Galatians 6: 7-10

Introduction

Parson's Porch Books is delighted to present to you this series called *Sermons Matter*.

We believe that many of the best writers are pastors who take the role of preacher seriously. Week in, and week out, they exegete scripture, research material, write and deliver sermons in the context of the life of their particular congregation in their given community.

We further believe that sermons are extensions of Holy Scripture which need to be published beyond the manuscripts which are written for delivery each Sunday. Books serve as a vehicle for the sermon to continue to proclaim the Good News of the Morning to a broader audience.

We celebrate the wonderful occasion of the preaching event in Christian worship when the Pastor speaks, the People listen and the Work of the Church proceeds.

Take, Read, and Heed.

David Russell Tullock
Publisher
Parson's Porch Books

Looking for a Sign
Isaiah 7.10-16; Matthew 1.18-25

The fourth Sunday of Advent we light the candle of love. And yet we have these texts about signs and decisions and divine advice – and I'm not sure what to make of them in the light of the candle of love. I had a hard time seeing the light shining through these texts in the same way the light of peace shone through the texts for that week.

As we come into this last week before Christmas, since Christmas is on a Sunday this last Sunday of Advent really is the last rest area on the road to Christmas morning. I suspect that we are tired of waiting, tired of not jumping fully into the Christmas spirit, tired of singing *O Come, O Come Emmanuel* and wishing we could all just get on with it. And frankly, that's what I heard in these texts this week. Let's get on with it.

King Ahaz is in a pickle. The enemy is camped outside, waiting to invade. And it will be bad. Very bad. And here comes the prophet, offering the King a gift: The Lord wants to give you a sign. Ask for a sign. A big one.

And the king, being the pious, righteous ruler that he is says... that's okay. I don't need to test God. Let's just get on with it.

By the rules of being right – for we should not test God, scripture says – the king is right. But it did show a supreme lack of trust in God and God's prophet and God's message. To say nothing of God's ability to work in the lives of humans and perhaps guide the king's army to victory despite all odds. But the king decides he'd rather take his chances rather than get a clear sign from God about next steps.

How often do we do that ourselves? Decide we know the right moves, the right path, the right decision – what's best for everyone?

Discernment (seeking to know the will of God), is a murky, never finished process which can be frustrating and lead you in places you have no desire to go. Instead, we tend to seek the will of a god that will benefit the world we desire, the world where we are comfortable – rather than seeking the will of a God that seeks to upend the status quo and create new things.

But just like the pious king who will not test God, God still wants to show us what could be – and so we get a sign anyway. We just may not understand it. Or want it, frankly. Because a new thing from a God of new things could have an option that would require us to change – to do something uncomfortable, out of the ordinary, something audacious.

And none of us want to change.

Now, contrast the pious king Ahaz with the carpenter Joseph.

Joseph has a problem.

His betrothed, Mary, has just told him she's pregnant, and has an unbelievable story to go along with it. And Joseph, being a good man, makes the kindest decision available to him: he'll divorce her and get on with things. Move on. Cut his losses but save Mary from the death sentence that would be the other option he had.

Then an angel shows up with a third, previously unconsidered option.

Joseph doesn't want to change any more than I do, and to do what the angel suggests means that he must go against a lifetime of teaching about the law – the law given by God, in fact – of what is right and wrong. Go against the advice of his friends, his family, his religious leaders. To take the angel's advice, Joseph had to give up his notions of comfort, of social conventions, perhaps even the dream of having time with his young bride alone before starting a family.

Joseph would have been absolutely within his rights – and within the letter and spirit of the law – to move ahead with his plan to divorce Mary and do it quietly so as not to make any more problem for her than necessary. But Joseph, unlike the pious king Ahaz, heard the word of the Lord, discerned the will of the Lord – and changed. Changed his mind, changed his plan, changed the trajectory of his life.

A simple carpenter from Nazareth would soon find himself on the run toward Egypt, having caught the notice of an evil king. I'm pretty sure that in the middle of that trip Joseph had to stop and wonder for a moment whether he had done the right thing in hearing that angel out.

Because hearing and doing the new things of God can be risky to the way we think things are, the way things ought to be, the right way, the legal way, the way of life we've known. In the world of signs from God, the rich and successful are… not. The poor deserve more. The first become last. Swords become plows. And in the ultimate irony, the meek inherit the earth.

But what does this have to do with the candle of love, you ask?

And rightly so. So, I offer this: we tend to get caught up in the ought to's – especially in this season. We ought to get our tree up and make it look great. We ought to get presents for all these folks. We ought to do this, cook that, see them…. In a season dedicated to peace and hope, we spend a great deal of time trying to navigate family dynamics, office politics, social rules and everyone's expectations. And none of that brings us one whit closer to peace or hope, much less understanding or love.

I digress: here's what I have to offer, courtesy of the prophet Bono – in a world where we tend to think first about what the "right" option is, we need to remember that love is a higher law.

Joseph was right in his plan to divorce Mary quietly – it was kind, it was legal, it would have restored him to a life he could count on. But, in the end, he chose the option that was not a legal option, but instead followed the higher law of love, which in the end, is the law that God expects us to follow.

We live in a world where the kind option is often not really an option. What sort of world would it be if instead of putting our faith in what is right and wrong, we put our faith into a God that loves us, loves others, and expects us to love others the same way. Instead, like the pious king Ahaz, we decide we know what God wants, expects, and out of that create policies and plans that have a one size fits all approach, we instead were to look at people individually. What if we treated troublesome neighbors as Joseph treated Mary - with love that went beyond right and wrong and kindness and moved into a place that took us out of town on the run?

The candle of love on this last Sunday of Advent should make us stop and think about the implications of a loving God that may push us into doing things we might not have considered. Make us change direction. Change course. Change.

So, we light the candle of love. And wait. For the change to come. And that may make us uncomfortable. Make us want to just get on with it. Move on. But the warm love light slows us down, bids us listen and wait for the sign. Bids us change….

New Year, New Resolutions

Matthew 2.13-23

We have a unique opportunity today – Starting a new year as we gather for worship on the Lord's Day. That happens about once every six years, so it's not unheard of, but still a good opportunity to take a deep breath and a good look around.

If you get your news of the outside world from the usual sources, 2017 will either be the end of nearly a decade of bad decisions and situations and the beginning of a renaissance, or the end of life as we know it. If you focus on celebrities, 2016 has been a bad year, especially for icons of the late baby boomer era. Generally, the overall mood is that we are all ready to bid adieu to 2016 and say bonjour to 2017. Some with resigned sighing. Some with a bit of jubilation. But ready to get on with the new things.

After the busyness of Christmas – and frankly, even I, who loves Christmas, was ready to be done – New Years can seem like a time to get a new start, a new outlook, a new gym membership, and move into something new.

This week's scripture isn't a new beginning – in fact it's a terrifying scene in the ongoing story of God's work with and for humans.

And it's a hard story. Hard after the waiting and preparation of Advent, with the soft candlelight and the talk of peace and love. Hard to put into context of the gentleness of the nativity story out of Luke. Hard to put into context when we talk about God working for the flourishing of all. Just hard.

This story, this the passage from Matthew's gospel, shows the new family, having just been visited by the three wise men from the East, on the run. Refugees, if you will. Fleeing for their lives into another country – undocumented if you will.

Meanwhile, back in Judea, Herod has decided that if he can't locate this child the wise men sought, all the male infants would have to go, just to be on the safe side. Because there was no way to properly vet those children and he couldn't take a chance. If any of them were a threat, then all of them were a threat.

So as a result, we have, embedded in this story of divine intervention to save the life of the child of Mary, what's referred to as the slaughter of the innocents.

And we must ask ourselves: If God was going to intervene, couldn't God have intervened to save all those babies? Why did so many others have to die so that Jesus would be spared. And if God could intervene to save Jesus, why did Joseph have to pack up his family in a hurry and head to Egypt, of all places. Ironically enough, the place where God brought his people OUT OF is now the place God sends the beloved of his people IN TO.

To save a little time this morning, I'm going to skip ahead and let you know I have no idea how to answer those questions. I have no idea why events played out as they did, why an all-powerful God did not intervene to stop the evil deed of an equally evil king. Matthew offers up this prophecy of Rachel crying for her children, but even to the scholars that wrote the commentaries I consulted this week as I looked for an answer to that question, it sounds a bit forced as to the fulfillment of prophecy.

What is clear is that we have moved from the silent night of Bethlehem, and into the weeping and wailing of a people once again visited by violence and death. I could offer up all sorts of theological constructs as to why this had to happen as it did, why this violence was perpetuated in order that the savior might be saved so that he could be the savior. But ultimately, in a world where we have cataloged so many horrors this past calendar year, I can't find the right words to adequately explain that kind of violence. Any more than I can find words that explain how leaders in Syria can do to their own people what has been done in Aleppo. Or in South Sudan.

Or in the past in various Latin American countries. Or in Germany in the 30's. Or Cambodia in the 70's and 80's.

Here's what I do think about this story this morning: it's a reminder to us that even though Jesus has come, things aren't done. There is still plenty of evil in this world. There is the massive, large scale evil that leads to the world's largest refugee camps where rape and starvation are the norm. And there is the smaller, more localized evil that leads to us believing that one human being is somehow more "deserving" or less equal than another based on nothing more than the color of their skin or the creed of their faith. Or lack of faith.

The story of God's work of salvation, fulfilled in the life, death and resurrection of Jesus plays out not in the safe and cloistered world of the stable in Bethlehem. It plays out in a world where God's people had to be delivered out of slavery. In a world where the Roman Empire nearly slaughtered all the Jews to stamp out rebellion. In a world where each of the twelve closest associates of Jesus – despite their bumbling and lack of understanding while Jesus was with them – died a martyr's death as witness to the beginning of something they could not imagine.

Our world is still a world where other humans are treated as property. Where large scale genocide happens at least once a decade – and we hardly notice any longer. Sometimes it may be hard to see that God is still working.

The story of the flight from Egypt is, at the core, a story of the continued obedience of Joseph and Mary. The angel said go. They went. They didn't stick around to try and figure out the whys and wherefores of the situation. They didn't wait.

Because the waiting of Advent is over. The pause to celebrate the coming of the king is over – now there are things that need to be done. The child was saved – and we should pay close attention to what that saved to save Jesus taught. It must have been important.

Jesus was continually talking about the kingdom of heaven – not as something we should be waiting and preparing for, but as something we should emulate. Jesus taught we should protect those who need protecting – regardless of their sin, as with the woman caught in adultery. Jesus taught that we should respect and engage those of different faiths, as with the woman at the well. Jesus taught that we should forgive those who do not deserve it, as with the prodigal son.

Jesus' death and resurrection are important – but his life was saved from Herod, so his LIFE was also important. Important in teaching us how to understand and emulate the kingdom of God. If we can't get behind the teachings of Jesus in the sermon on the mount now, we are going to be very unhappy in the kingdom to come when the underserving and the meek are at the head of the crowd.

The prophet Micah told the children of Israel: What does God require of humans? To do justice, to love mercy, and to walk humbly with God. Jesus' life showed us how those things work with real people.

Our liturgical year is framed by the birth, death and resurrection of Jesus. In between those times, we have "Ordinary Time." And because it's ordinary, we may tend to dismiss it. But I think the story this morning, for all it's troubling questions we can't answer, warns us not to dismiss the things between the birth and death of Jesus. That life was saved. God could have redeemed the world in any manner – but chose instead to send the beloved one to show us how to live a life.

We should pay attention to that life and what it teaches us about our own life. And what we should pay attention to.

I don't really make new years' resolutions, but I think that would be a good one – to pay more attention truly to what Jesus would do, and like Joseph, just get up and do it.

The Order of the Law

Matthew 5.21-37

I am a fan of *Law and Order*. The original *Law and Order*. *Criminal Intent*. Even *SVU* for a while, but lately not so much. I've even watched the British version. I honestly think it's the title that's appealing: *Law. And Order.* People following the rules. Sticking to the plan. And when they don't there are consequences. It's straightforward. No need for creative thinking, thinking outside the box, or winging it.

Which is pretty much how the Law of God plays out, right? Straightforward, consequences, easy to figure out and no need to have any deep thinking to apply it. That's the deal with a law: it says what it says and that's it.

So, if that's true, how in the world have we gotten to a place where there are so many ways to interpret the law – not just of God, but of the laws we make ourselves. We're watching multiple dramas play out in our own country about what happens when something that seems straightforward suddenly isn't. And how different people can see the same words on a page and come to completely different conclusions.

This was happening, even in Jesus' time, with the Law as given to Moses at Sinai. You had the Pharisees. The Scribes. The Sadducees. The Essenes. And even more, smaller groups. And each of these groups read and interpreted the same words – but came to slightly different conclusions. The Pharisees, for instance, held that strict following of the law, the letter of the law, was most important. And they came up with books and books of interpretation that addressed nearly every human situation and what you should do. The Sadducees on the other hand, were more interested in the spirit of the law. So, it stands to reason that the Sadducees were more involved in politics – in cooperating with the Roman Empire. During Jesus' time, referred to as Second Temple Judaism, there was no shortage of rabbis in synagogues interpreting the law, helping people to live lives in according to God's design.

And along comes Jesus of Nazareth, a rabbi who isn't welcome in his own town because of his sermons. And he has a following – literally, people following him wherever he wanders. And because he hasn't a synagogue of his own, he preaches in places like on hill. And says things like blessed are the meek....

And this morning, we get to the heart of Jesus' interpretation of the law. You have heard it said... And in the verse immediately preceding this, Jesus told those gathered that he did not come to abolish the law, but to fulfill it.

Now I don't know if you are familiar with the full law Jesus was referring to, but the Ten Commandments were the start. If you really want a hoot of a weekend sometime, read all of Leviticus and Deuteronomy. And then we'll talk about wearing clothes of two different fabrics and the merits of Shrimpfest at Red Lobster. But I digress....

The fact was and is this – the Law as given to Moses was hard. It's unlikely that anyone could go their entire lives and not break some part of it at some point. And the words of Moses, in his farewell speech before the children of Israel moved into the Promised Land:

> [15]*See, I have set before you today life and prosperity, death and adversity.* [16]*If you obey the commandments of the LORD your God that I am commanding you today, by loving the LORD your God, walking in his ways, and observing his commandments, decrees, and ordinances, then you shall live and become numerous, and the LORD your God will bless you in the land that you are entering to possess.* [17]*But if your heart turns away and you do not hear but are led astray to bow down to other gods and serve them,* [18]*I declare to you today that you shall perish; you shall not live long in the land that you are crossing the Jordan to enter and possess.*

And in Jesus day there was an overwhelming belief that if you were suffering from some disease, defect, financial reversal, well, these things were proof that you were out of sync with God's law. And we tend to sort of believe that today – what goes around comes around. Karma. Reap what you sow.

But when the rabbi Jesus sat down on that hill to interpret the law for those gathered around him, he put a new spin on it. Well, not new, but a reminder of why the law was given in the first place.

You have heard it said…. and then Jesus offers up his interpretation on the law ranging from murder to adultery to divorce, to keeping your word, and telling the truth. And I suspect that in many cases, rabbis interpreted the law to narrow it so that more could follow it. This is where we get the notion of justifiable homicide. Little white lies. Lust is unavoidable.

Jesus, on the other hand, broadened the notion of the law. It's not wrong just to kill another person. Anger is also wrong. It's not wrong just to commit adultery. It's wrong to want to. For Jesus, the law went beyond the actual act – it went to intentions. To motivations. To the heart, in fact.

And I don't think Jesus chose these examples by accident. Believe me, there are plenty of things in Leviticus Jesus could have chosen to expand upon. But he seems to have deliberately chosen examples that combine to make a point Jesus made again and again in his ministry: relationships matter. People's lives matter. People matter. All of them. Especially those that are vulnerable – and those lives might need to matter just a little bit more to those who seek to live in the light of God.

Jesus uses the law not to kill to expand on how we deal with one another. Not only is it wrong to kill, but it's also wrong to allow ourselves to get so angry with another person that our words and actions are out of our control. As someone who spent a great deal of my life angry, I can attest to the fact that anger can control you and whisper in your ear that some absurd things make sense. Anger not addressed can lead us to warped relationships where we may believe the world is better off without certain people.

This is, friends, an angry world. Our politics are fueled by anger. Our religion is often fueled by anger. A certain amount of anger is good – it riles us up to address injustice, right wrongs, protect the vulnerable. But unchecked anger is not good. Undirected anger is very bad – and Jesus says not dealing with our anger, not repairing relationships, not seeing other humans as worthwhile in the eyes of God can lead us to a place where we have done as much damage as killing another. Maybe the damage is only to ourselves, but it's damage none the less.

There's a lot more to unpack in this passage this morning. We could talk more about how Jesus words on divorce were addressing the issue of men who treated women as property to be discarded on their word alone. We could talk about the issue of uncontrolled desire and how it can objectify others. We could talk about how the notion of "eye for an eye" justice was a limit on punishment in a brutal world where execution was the punishment for stealing a loaf of bread. We could talk about truth telling and promise keeping in a world where fake news and campaign promises evoke only a head shake and a chuckle.

It's right here that I need to warn you of a spoiler alert for next week: Jesus had an agenda for interpreting the law as he did. Not only did he want people to think less about what they could do and still be within in the law, he wanted them to think about why the law was given in the first place. Jesus was talking to the people, not to give them new laws, or new ways to comply with the law, but calling them into a new way of living that honored God's law, which first and foremost was given to help the children of Israel prosper in a strange land, to get along with each other (as they'd proven they were a bit contentious, at best), and to live within the will and light of God. And why did God give them this law? It was given out of love. Which, at the end of the day, is what it was all about anyway. The law was given to a new people on a new day to teach them a new way to live. Given by a loving father to children who needed structure.

If you've parented, or taught school, or been around children at all, you know that for toddlers, the rules must be straightforward, simple, and concise. Do not touch that.

By the time they are teenagers, the rules can be more complex: Don't touch that unless there is a fire. There's some agency granted. And for adults, the rules tend to take on less of a negative: if there's a fire, grab that. Lots of agency, lots of personal accountability.

Jesus was assuming that the folks he was talking to desire more than the simple "thou shalt not" rules given to the brand-new people headed into a brand-new land. He was asking the people not just to line up their behavior to conform to a set of rules and regulations. He was asking them to line up their hearts to conform to the heart of a God that loves them – so that they might love others. Jesus said this a few chapters later in Matthew:

> 'YOU SHALL LOVE THE LORD YOUR GOD WITH ALL YOUR HEART, AND WITH ALL YOUR SOUL, AND WITH ALL YOUR MIND.' 38 "This is the great and foremost commandment. 39 "The second is like it, 'YOU SHALL LOVE YOUR NEIGHBOR AS YOURSELF.' 40 "On these two commandments depend the whole Law and the Prophets."

I have heard it put this way: Jesus puts forth the love command as the key to the Scriptures. The prophet Bono puts it this way: Love is a higher law.

Jesus is calling us, not to new ways of living out an episode of Law and Order, but to a new way of being, and new way of living, a new way of seeing the world and the people in it. Or as Moses puts it: a choice between life and death, light and dark. Both for us and the world. Let us always choose light and life.

There's a Light…
Isaiah 9.2-6; Luke 2.1-14

There's a Carpenter's Christmas song that begins: "The Christmas cards have all been sent… the Christmas rush is through." That's often the way I feel on Christmas Eve evening. That finally, the end of all the hurry up ding dings, the end of the buying frenzy, the end of the stress is all in sight. There is light at the end of the tunnel. Which would imply we have been on a forced march through a tunnel rather than on a journey of preparation for peace and love.

There IS light on this night – a light that shines in the darkness, but I often think we mistake that light for the end of that tunnel – possibly even an oncoming train – rather than the soft light that eventually conquers the darkness.

I've been afraid of the dark most of my life – it's not cool to admit that. I'm better, but given the chance to turn on a light, I will nearly always do it. The dark is full of unknown things that could be dangerous, could be painful – things to fear. Even the very familiar takes on an ominous edge in the dark. And Isaiah was writing to folks who most definitely were NOT surrounded by the familiar. They were over-run, captive. There was plenty of darkness.

There is plenty of darkness in the world we inhabit as well. Plenty to fear, plenty that can't be known. Whether it's fear of terrorists – whose very name tells you that their main job is to make us afraid – or fear of economic changes, or fear of life transitions – we age, our children grow up and out of our houses, we change or lose jobs: there is so much that can look like either a way out, or more oncoming danger.

But the prophet says this: the people who have been in darkness have seen a light. A great light. A light that shows the truth to the world. And that truth was shouted from heaven on a dark night in Bethlehem: Fear Not! For there is good news. Good news for everybody, not just a few. Not just the powerful, those with enough status and money to work the system. Not for the ones who overachieve. Not just for the ones that pull themselves up by their bootstraps – but even for the ones that have no bootstraps. Good news for all people.

And this light, this good news, comes into the world in a most unexpected way: a child. Born nobody in the middle of nowhere.

There is another Christmas song that comes to me on Christmas eve: the second verse of "O Little Town of Bethlehem." It begins this way: "how silently, how silently the wondrous gift is given. So, God imparts to human hearts the blessings of his heaven."

For this light is a wondrous gift.

When you've been afraid – truly afraid of the dark, you learn this: the only thing the light does is change what you see, not what is. For the children of Israel in Isaiah's time, the promise of the light didn't change the fact that the enemy was camped outside the gates, waiting to overrun them. And for Joseph and Mary, it didn't change the fact that they were a long way from home due to the whims of a government to whom they were merely numbers; uncomfortable, having their first child in less than optimal circumstances. For the shepherds on the hill that dark night, the great light of the heavenly host proclaiming the good news did not change the fact that on the ladder of their world, they were likely not even on a rung, much less a higher rung than most. The light that was wondrously given that night in Bethlehem didn't appear to change much of anything. But it changed everything.

Light changes what we see, and how we react to it. Light can kill the things that harm us and nurture the things that help us. Light can dispel fear by diminishing those fears – getting rid of the shadows, illuminating the weakness of the things that would harm us, and empowering us to step more confidently, stand taller, breathe deeper.

The light that came into the world, to a people living in darkness – that light has the power to transform, just as turning on the light makes the fear filled darkness into an easily navigated place. Not by magically giving us new circumstances, but by providing the hope and love that empowers us to move through now, to get to the later, and eventually to the promised later where all is made right.

The gospel of John tells us that the light that came into the world was the Word of God – which was God. When you strip all the things away that will bring light and life and transformation into the world, the place where Jesus himself started – it's with words. Words that are kind. Words that lift rather than tear down. Words that point out the dignity of all humans, rather than the differences between us. All that begins with words, words that are kind. What would change in my life, your life, the world in general, if we chose to see the light and be, first and foremost, kind to one another?

That's a lot of expectation on a winter's night. But as we'll see in just a few minutes, the light that came into the world on that silent night – the light represented by this one candle – can spread. And as the light spreads, bringing the Word and inspiring our words – the darkness is dispelled. And it's not just a metaphor – every extra bit of light in the world makes one less shadow, one less fear, one more word of Grace and love.

We prepare to come to this table, a table where we celebrate this gift of light, of hope, of grace. This is a table where we come to be fed, to remember, and to celebrate the light that came to us as we dwell in darkness. To remember there is good news to be shared. So, let us celebrate the light – remember the gift – and come to this table knowing there is grace and love here, and plenty to share.

Bread, Bath, and Beyond [1]

Mark 1.4-11

Today is Baptism of the Lord Sunday – that Sunday that marks the end of Christmas, and the beginning of the short period of ordinary time before Ash Wednesday and Lent. While it hardly seems possible that we could be anywhere close to thinking about Lent and Easter, the church year, like everything else, marches on. Star Trek fans – despite the feeling that we've been here before, there has been no anomaly in the space time continuum. It just seems that way.

Time is a funny thing, though. And if you ever do any reading about theories of time, (and I don't encourage it if you are at all susceptible to brain cramps that lead to migraines) you may find that there are theories of time, philosophies of time – and they add up to this: our sense of time is just that – a sense. The reality of time is something that subjective, and any school kid who's waited for that last bell, or anyone who's sat through a long staff meeting knows that sometimes an hour is the shortest time possible and sometimes it's all day.

So, in some ways it seems like we were just at this point in the year, and in some ways, we were. And here we are again. Hearing the story – this time from the gospel of Mark – of Jesus seeking out John the Baptist at the river Jordan and asking to be baptized. Launching his public ministry, beginning the inexorable journey toward Jerusalem that brings him and his followers to that same place we find ourselves in just a matter of weeks – at the table, at the cross, at the tomb.

Jesus's baptism marks the point where things change for him, for the world – for the story of God's work in the world. Just like when the Israelites were in the wilderness and God called Moses up to the mountain and told him that this group of people, from that point

---

[1] I shamelessly stole this title from a colleague, the Rev. Dr. David Gambrell, Office of Theology and Worship, Presbyterian Church (USA).

on, would be called God's people, this baptism marks a new way for God to deal with humans.

In those technical terms you learn to use in seminary, what happens in the river Jordan that morning is that God condescends to mortals. And that word needs some explanation – condescending is not something that we want to be on the receiving end of, right? But in the true nature of the word, something important is happening.

Remember the story of the tower of Babel? Humans decided they would build a tower that would take them up to heaven and into the presence of God. And it didn't work out so well. In fact, that's not the only time humans have tried to second guess God in the history of the world, but the Babel story is important because it shows us a couple of things: that people don't tend to know their own limitations; that humans often get the relationship between God and mortals wrong; and God does things in our best interest that often are misconstrued by humans. But the biggest point of Babel is this: humans can't, can't, can't move from their place in the mortal world upward into the presence of God. Can't be done.

So, because we cannot overcome our humanity and move onto an equal plane with God, God had to do something.

The Old testament passage for today is the creation story from Genesis: God moving over the waters and creating something from nothing, making light where there was only dark. And then, after creating the world God created humans – to be in relationship. We were created to be in relationship with God and with each other from the very beginning.

Here's the thing about relationships – there is no such thing as a fifty/fifty relationship. Relationships tend to be a dance of giving and receiving – at least the healthy ones are. Whether we're talking about friendship, marriages, work relationships, church relationships, there must be a balance of giving and receiving. And in any relationship, there is not equality in abilities or gifts or interests, and good relationships recognize that. The trick is to understand who you are, who the other person is, and build your relationship around the truth of that.

So, humans have not always been good at realizing that in a relationship with our creator, we haven't always been honest with ourselves about who we are and our role in the relationship. Take the Israelites in the wilderness – no more had God led them out of slavery in Egypt then the people began to forget. Here we are in the wilderness, nothing to eat but manna, nothing to drink but water from a rock. God's brought us out of the good life we had in Egypt and into this stinky ole wilderness. We can do better. So, they built themselves a God they liked better…

But it doesn't work that way. You can't be in relationship unless you can find a place at which the relationship can exist, and in the case of humans and God, we can't get to a place where that can happen. They had forgotten God had to come to the mountain to meet Moses.

In Jesus, we have the ultimate condescension of God to man – and by that, I mean that we reclaim the meaning of the word, which is to stoop or deign to do something: He would not condescend to misrepresent the facts.

OR

to put aside one's dignity or superiority voluntarily and assume equality with one regarded as inferior: He condescended to their intellectual level to be understood. (definition from Merriam-Webster.com)

In Jesus, God condescends to humans. Because we cannot move upward to be more like God, God came to us as us. And in the baptism of Jesus we see that this is announced, proclaimed and given to the world.

In most of the pictures/stories of Jesus' baptism, we see Jesus standing with water dripping down his face, looking upward as the dove settles on his head and the skies are beautiful, blue with the light of heaven shining down from an opening in the clouds. All is calm. All is bright.

But Mark's gospel doesn't say the heavens calmly parted – he says the heavens were ripped open. Torn open – the Greek word in the text is *Schizono*, the same word that gives us schizophrenic or schism. It's not a pretty word. When the heavens opened, were torn open, God then said, "this is my son," this is me, come to you. I'm happy, I'm pleased. Pay attention. And this comes from heavens that have been ripped open. This is a sign things have changed.

Consider if you will the lowly bag of potato chips – one of my special pet peeves is people who have no idea how to open a bag of potato chips. Chips get stale quickly, so you need to open the bag in such a way that it's easy to close it up and put one of those handy dandy clips on it. But some people are in such a hurry to open the bag that they end up putting a tear down the side where no incarnation of any kind of handy clip will keep the chips fresh.

This is what happened that day at the river Jordan – the barrier between God and humans was ripped in such a way that from that moment on, things were never going to be the same. God, through the Son, was now with us, standing in the river Jordan, walking with us and among us. We were, from this moment on, in a different kind of relationship with God. We no longer had to try and find a way to get from here to heaven…. It was done for us. God CONDESCENDED to us.

The waters of baptism are the place where we can hear the rippling of the waters of creation, the place where we are reminded that we are in relationship to the creator – we the creation are able to know and be known by the creator.

Mary Shelley wrote the book *Frankenstein*, which is about the desire of a creature to be loved by the creator. In that story, the doctor who created the creature did not know or understand what he had created. The creature's unfulfilled longing to be loved by the creator ended in disaster. The creature could not be what Frankenstein was, and Frankenstein was appalled by what he had created.

Despite what Mary Shelley and her companions may have thought, this is not the story of our relationship to our creator. Our creator has a longing to know and be known by us and has taken the extraordinary step of becoming one of us in order to truly know and be known. This is exemplified in the story of Jesus' baptism.

John didn't want to baptize Jesus – he didn't think he was the right person to do it and didn't think Jesus needed baptism. About that he was right – the baptism was done for our sake, to make the point that God was here, with us **as** us. And nothing was ever going to be the same.

Baptism should change things, so they can never be like they were again – not the actual act of baptism, of course. But the knowledge of baptism, the reality of knowing that we are claimed by God, named by God, known by God and can truly know and experience God – this should be life changing. Should color what we do. Make us better – and better able to be in relationship with God.

This baptism represents a kind of crossroads in the history of God's dealings with humans. John the Baptist stands as a prophet – the kind that brought God's message to the people in the past. He stands in the wilderness: the place where the people were led by God. And Jesus – God with us – comes to that place, to that prophet and in that moment; the past of wilderness and prophet is linked forever to the future and the glimpse into heaven. That is not the last day in the wilderness, nor is it the day when heaven fully comes down and the kingdom is fulfilled. But it's the point at which the two are, if only for a moment, linked, joined and can be seen together. The despair of wilderness and captivity will eventually be left behind. The wonders of the kingdom will eventually be a reality. And the promise of those things is bound up in this one man, this dripping person who stands in the water as he begins a journey toward Jerusalem. The pain and suffering have not ended. But in the river that day, we are given the gift of knowing that wilderness, pain and suffering are not the last word. God gets the last word.

And it will end well. For God is well pleased.

Come and See

1 Samuel 3.1-10; John 1.43-51

Can anything good come out of Nazareth? With that question, Nathaniel verbalizes the mystery of the incarnation. Can the things that redeem us, save us, heal us, bind us together – can these things come from places that we don't expect. Or respect?

And if we aren't open to the places things can come from do we run the risk of missing the message, missing the call? If we aren't open to the discernment that comes from our friends and fellow disciples, might we miss something important?

Before we get to that question – can anything good come from... wherever, there is the story of Samuel's call.

Here's the thing about a call from God: it is personal, calls us by name, assumes that God knows us, knows the situation, and doesn't always include the mandate to go forth and preach repentance. Samuel hears a call – but doesn't know who is calling or why. The priest Eli, who, along with his corrupt sons, had become nearly useless, finally recognizes that the God who no longer speaks directly to him is now speaking to his young apprentice. There is a lot to unpack in there – knowing when to know to let go, the personal issues created by Eli having to turn over the work to this youngster, but also that Eli has a new job helping Samuel be prepared.

So, Eli instructs Samuel to answer the call by saying: speak Lord, your servant is listening.

Far too often, I think we hear a call from God and believe that we must immediately know exactly how that all should be, and that we see the full journey; that once we hear the call, the need for discernment is over. I've known people who respond to God's call with: I'm here, I'm on the way, I'm out to evangelize, to pepper the town with the good news, to volunteer for the mission field. The respond with an action plan and annual goals.

But sometimes, if we waited and listened for more, we might find that our call is something much less dramatic. For Samuel, he was given the message that Eli and his sons would be brought down, but not told that it was his responsibility to deliver that message. He was told so that Samuel would know what his work was.

"Speak, Lord. Your servant is listening."

What might God be saying in the quiet to us? That there are children who need to be loved? That there are young people looking for a place to ask questions about life and faith? That there are folks who are lonely and need little more than a phone call now and then? Or a card?

There is lots in this call story of Samuel, but this morning, I'd like you to remember this: our response to God's ongoing call should not be promises of what we will and will not do, but rather a promise to listen, to continue to listen in and among all the transitions and changes of life. We don't have to know exactly how things are going to turn out, have all the details nailed down, be able to visualize the journey from beginning to end. We only must be willing to listen and take the next step.

We often think God calls us to be the bishop on the chess board, able to move the entire diagonal of the board, or the rook, able to move the width and length. But, God usually calls us to be more like the pawn – moving only one block at a time, not responsible for the full strategy, but an integral part of it. I find some comfort in that – that I only need to see the next step, not the next twenty....

Being able to see the next step is the story of Philip and Nathaniel.

John's gospel is focused on Jesus' identity. And in this short passage, there are multiple ways Jesus is identified: the fulfillment of Moses' law; the fulfillment of prophecy; rabbi; son of God; king of Israel. (There are others, but you get the picture) So there is this question moving underneath the text here: who is this Jesus? And in this, we get this short vignette with Philip and Nathaniel. Nathaniel the scoffer.

Can anything good come from Nazareth, he asks?

I fear we have come to a place in our world when we ask a version of that question far too often. Can anything good come from liberals? Can anything good come from conservatives? Can anything good come from progressive theology? Can anything good come from "over there?" Can anything good come from.... and you can insert your sentence finisher here.

And I think that most of the world is asking this morning: can anything good come from church, from religion, from Christianity? And we have only ourselves to blame – the church tends to do harm by not listening when God speaks, to protect the institution, too long to be a powerful force in the world. And along the way, we have both missed part of the message/the call and missed opportunities to share the call.

If you ever watched the show West Wing, there's an episode that's a flashback of how some of the president's team joined him. Sam Seaborn is a corporate attorney who has abandoned working on political campaigns because he is cynical about the worth of candidates. His friend Josh calls him and tells him he's going to New Hampshire to see a governor speak, and he thinks he might be "the real deal." And he makes Sam promise that if Josh comes back and tells him this governor is "the real deal," that Sam will join the campaign. Next scene: Sam is in a board room, arguing the tiny words in a very long contract when he sees Josh's face in the window. And Josh is nodding yes. Sam immediately gets up and leaves the board room, quitting his job as he goes.

I suspect Philip and Nathaniel might have had a similar deal. Philip doesn't try to argue with his friend, try to change his mind. He just says: come and see. This guy is the real deal.

Come and see. We aren't supposed to bring people to Christ by arguing the merits of believing. By offering them something – whether that's an easier life now or a mansion in heaven later. We're supposed to have something for them to see – see that life following Jesus is filled with joy, hope, love, light, companionship, grace, gratitude, meaning. Come and See.

I ran across this quote yesterday from writer Madeleine L'Engle: *we do not draw people to Christ by loudly discrediting what they believe, by telling them how wrong they are and how right we are, but by showing them a light that is so lovely that they want with all their hearts to know the source of it."* (*Walking on Water,* Waterbrook Press, 1980*)*

Nathaniel, who did come and see, saw and heard that Jesus was the real deal. Cynical, scoffing Nathaniel saw, and then he listened. Speak lord, your servant is listening.

As we go out into the world, I suspect we would all be better off with more listening and less talking. But I also think the world would be better off if we encouraged people to come and see – come and see the difference that Christ makes in us, in our community, in our ability to hope rather than fear. Come and see.

And we must have something to show them – rather than just tell them.

So – can anything good come out of the places we find ourselves?

I think the answer is yes – always yes. Come and see….

I Love a Parade
Luke 19.28-40

There's nothing like a good parade, don't you think? Parades large and small can draw a crowd, bring out the lawn chairs, and create a shortage of tissue paper. Parades make a STATEMENT – in a way that other things can't accomplish so efficiently. We have them before big things – like football games. And after big things – like winning the world series. And today, the last stop in our Lent journey, Jesus arrives in Jerusalem, and there's a parade.

Parades into Jerusalem weren't that big a deal. Happened all the time. Because you know why parades started, right? To show off.

Where I grew up, parades included the fire trucks, the police cars, the best convertibles the town had to offer. And every organization, church, or scout troop had a float on a wagon. A show of the things that protect us, serve us, tell people who we are. The Roman Empire may not have been the first people to do parades, but they had made them a kind of art form.

The Roman Empire intended to be "the" empire, and they kept the peace – Pax Romana, the peace of Rome. And they kept the peace through frequent sabre rattling and parades of force. They would come through the main gate of the city, with all their weapons – like the catapults – followed by the soldiers with swords, horses, and armor. And those chariots – remember that movie Ben Hur? That chariot scene still haunts my dreams.

When the Romans arrived in town, they would have all the military equipment, horses, chariots, artillery, soldiers in armor – all lined up and moving through the streets of town. It was how they showed who was in charge. And following all the show of power would be the spoils of war – the treasure, the food, the women. And then, in chains, would be the men they had captured who would serve as slaves, or maybe fodder for the gladiator games. The parade was a show of might, strength – and served as a warning to anyone that might be considering pushing back against the power of the Roman empire. When the Romans came into town, they expected to come into town a make an impression – and leave no doubt who was in charge, where the seat of power was, and how useless it was to attempt to fight back. Anyone not cheering on the Roman war machine would have been subject to a quick and merciless death.

The very same week that Jesus came into Jerusalem riding on a colt, there could have been another parade into the city. Herod may have entered the city from the West, with all the power of the Roman empire before him, a show of power designed to ensure that during the Passover week, the Jews did not get out of hand. The message was clear – Rome is in charge, the emperor, and his minion Herod, are to be feared. Pax Romana – the peace of Rome – was good if you toed the Roman line. And if you didn't, one step out of line, and Pax Romana would be enforced with the full force and power of Roman Homeland Security.

Jesus comes into the city from the east, riding on a colt, not in a war chariot, and not with the show of power that comes from machines of war. Rather than designed to strike fear into the people, this parade instead causes the people to cheer, to herald the arrival with palms instead of weapons, with colorful cloaks spread on the ground before Jesus. The peace of heaven did not need to be enforced – in fact, Jesus told those who told him to keep it down that the peace of heaven would be proclaimed by the very earth. This parade had all the hallmarks of a party on the edge of getting out of hand.

Herod's entrance was designed to show who was boss. Jesus' entrance was designed to remind the people of the prophet's words, and the song of the psalmist. Blessed is the one, the king, who comes in the name of the Lord. Herod wanted to make sure this Passover went off without the people being reminded of anything other than the power of Rome. Jesus was there to make sure that the people remembered who was really in charge, that God was faithful, and God's love endures forever.

We live in a world where knowing who is in charge is important and showing who's in charge is a full-time job. Current events make clear that sabre rattling is not a lost art in the world. Just like Herod, the powers of the world parade their gadgets and weapons and flaunt their power, posturing and spinning and trying to prove they're the most powerful, the most right, the, well, the most. In our own government, the powers that be and the powers that wanna be are continually making statements, parading their power and ideas and position papers. And during all this, we fail to recognize what **is** peace and what **is** true power.

Whatever Palm Sunday is, it's a time of contrast and contradictions. The contrast between the parade of power and might coming through the west gate and the parade of children and palms coming in the east gate. The contradiction between the hosannas that greet Jesus' arrival and the cries for blood that will soon ring out in the same city. Perhaps even from the same voices.

A contrast between triumphant entry and the humiliation of crucifixion. The contradiction of the ruler of the universe riding on a borrowed colt rather than a war chariot. Between the austere journey of Lent and the loud shouts of welcome. Between the conflict of this world and the peace of heaven.

But the biggest contrast is this: that the kingdom of God, unlike the kingdoms of this world, is not dependent on the spectacle of the show of power, the wealth of the spoils of war, the ability to take prisoners. The kingdom of God is instead dependent on the shouts of children and the unimportant; the borrowed colt that signals humility rather than power; the coming in the back gate rather than the main door; the inclusion of everyone, not just those who have access to power and wealth.

Today is a contrast between two parades. Which of those are we watching, paying attention to?

Truthfully, the parade of power and influence is a lot more fun to watch. It's entertaining – and more comfortable and maybe more comforting – to see the show of power that will protect us. Keep the peace. And if there are folks that get caught on the wrong side of that power, well, it's not us. We're still safely on the sidelines of the parade.

The other parade, the one coming in the side gate, needs people taking part in the parade, laying down colorful cloaks, waving palms, shouting. The parade of the powerful sends the message that power must be protected at any cost. And will be. The parade of the humble sends the message that the real power doesn't rest with the powerful. It's a paradox.

You can't be at both parades. So which parade for you on this Palm Sunday? The parade of the powerful, the ones in charge, the show of force? Or the smaller parade that is a show of humility, of service, of walking into the danger zone with nothing more than a borrowed donkey and some palm fronds as weapons? One promises Pax Romana – peace at any cost and the security for a way of life. The other promises peace that passes understanding and life eternal.

The parade of power, coming in the main gate to make a statement, is designed to keep the peace, maintain order, and whispers in our ear "it's best this way." The parade of Christ, on the other hand, is subversive, comes in the back way, and rejects the notion of going along to get along. Jesus says that if that parade hadn't happened, the very stones of the earth would have proclaimed the hosannas of the peace of heaven. As we go forth from this place, which parade are we in?

There's always a bigger crowd at the bigger parade. It's exciting, has lots to see, lots of impressive things. It leads to the seductive courtyard of safety and security. The smaller parade is less attractive, less exciting – but invites everyone to take part. The problem is: this parade leads directly to the Upper Room, to the Garden of Gethsemane, to Calvary.

Two parades. Two ways of seeing the world – which do we claim? Moving into Holy Week, let us choose wisely.

From Palm Sunday to Good Friday
Mark 1.1-11

Who doesn't love Palm Sunday? After the long, difficult journey of Lent, the celebration of Palm Sunday is as welcome as the blooming of the tulips after a long winter. (not that we'd know at this point)

For the last several weeks we've been journeying with Jesus toward Jerusalem and the fate that awaits him – and suddenly, we get to sing hosanna, and proclaim triumph. But as any University of Kentucky basketball fan can tell you this time of year, it isn't wise to celebrate too early, because there is still more to the story.

One of the things you get to do when you are in a high school band, is be in parades. In my case, lots of them. And you see the back side of parades – the parts that aren't all throwing candy and waving while wearing tiaras. Our band marched at Disney World once, and the set up for the parade there was brutal, long, hot – and not fun. But the folks on the street leading down to the castle didn't see any of that – they just saw the parade.

Mark gives us more information on the parade preparation this morning than he does about the actual parade. Jesus seemed deliberate about all this – about how he would come into the city and have that entrance make a statement. Which is odd, because mostly in Mark's gospel, Jesus told his followers to keep quiet about who he is and what he'd done. But this time, this close to the end of the journey, Jesus is ready to come out and be known.

And not only does that make him visible to the powers that be, it also creates a situation where the people had to decide – do we follow, do we get on board? And the palm leaves began to wave, and the cheering got loud. This small imitation of the power parades of victorious military leaders came in the side gate of the city, had the leader riding on a colt rather than a stallion, and had women and children cheering rather than being intimidated by the show of power. And then, once the parade was over, Jesus, rather than having a victory party, looked around a bit and then went back out to Bethany. To his friends' house, where Mary, Martha, and Lazarus lived.

Jesus gave his disciples explicit directions to prepare for his entrance into the city – and being the dunderheads that they were, they thought this was IT – the time when Jesus would finally reveal the big plan to liberate Israel from the bootheel of Rome, restore the land, restore the kingship of David. To finally get it all together, bind up the wounds, declare victory. But after all the preparation, he comes in, looks around, and then goes to hang out with his friends.

Because Jesus knew what we know: that the same people who would be waving palms and shouting Hosanna on the streets that day, would, in a very short period, be the same people shouting out "crucify him, crucify him!" The very same voices that cried out "blessed is the one that comes in the name of the Lord," would soon cry out that they preferred Barabbas the thief. This same Jesus, who entered the city to shouts of joy and in a parade of triumph, would, in a matter of days, be subjected to humiliation, and pain, and death.

It's tempting to separate Palm Sunday from the reality of Holy Week – but Holy Week, the week of pain and separation and betrayal, begins here. The triumph of Jesus is bound up in the humiliation of Jesus, and if we separate the two, we are doing a disservice to both. Dietrich Bonhoeffer, the theologian executed by the Nazis, said we are tempted to embrace a cheap grace – a grace that celebrates the divinity of Jesus and his triumph over death, while ignoring the humanity of Jesus, the embodiment of love and obedience that sets the example we are to follow.

I spent last weekend at a conference where a variety of speakers addressed the question of why follow Jesus in a time where, 2000 plus years after Jesus' birth, we seem to be no further along on the road to redemption. What difference does it make to be a follower of Christ? What difference does it make that this humble rabbi who entered the city in triumph would soon be executed in bitter defeat?

There are some who might answer the question with some variation of these: to go to heaven when you die; to have an abundant life, whatever that might mean, whether it's success, or money, or power, or just contentment; to share in the gifts of grace and love; to be a better person; to be happier; because it's the right thing to do.

But the folks that answered that question last week – as I dare say Dietrich Bonhoeffer as well – did not answer with any of those things. Each of them answered from a place of deep pain and woundedness – and each of them answered it this way: the pain and humiliation of the incarnation of God in Jesus spoke to their own pain and woundedness and made them see the pain of others and want to offer a balm. We sang, over and over, "there is a balm in Gilead that makes the wounded whole" – and to sing that song in the space between Palm Sunday and Good Friday seems both right and needed. The assurance that grace is not cheap – that it is gifted to us by a God that understands pain and humiliation – and that the gift of grace is for this life at this time, for us and for others: this assurance is why I am a follower of Christ. For as one of the speakers said last week: it's all fine and good to sing about the sweet by and by, but friends, I need a little something before I die.

If we are going to follow a savior who goes headlong into the danger, straight into the places where death waits – we better be surrounded by grace that will give us a little something now, strengthen us for this journey in addition to preparing us for the life that awaits.

The epistle lesson for this Sunday is Philippians 2.5-11: Paul tells the church this:

> *Let the same mind be in you that was in Christ Jesus, who, though he was in the form of God, did not regard equality with God as something to be exploited, but emptied himself, taking the form of a slave, being born in human likeness. And being found in human form, he humbled*

> *himself and became obedient to the point of death – even death on a cross.*

As we line up for the parade today, it would behoove us not to forget that there is a direct path from Palm Sunday to Good Friday, and that those of us waving the palms today will be calling for blood by the end of the week, denying Christ before the rooster crows, and wondering how things could have changed so quickly. For to follow Christ – to be a Christian – means having the same willingness to go through Palm Sunday, knowing that Friday is coming. Knowing that our own dignity will be sacrificed on the altar of something much more important. But also knowing that our best life now is only possible when we have the same mind that is in Christ – and that the God that can heal our brokenness, who gifts us with grace, is the same God that understands what it is to be broken, brokenhearted, and wounded. This is the God that calls us to follow – not to stand on the side and wave palms, but to follow to the scary places we might be led. Follow the one that can sustain and nurture us whatever may come.

The psalms we have been reading this Lent, and studying on Wednesday evenings, say over and over: there is much to lament. But they also assure us that God is faithful, ever-loving, ever near to lift us up.

Remembering that, even with Good Friday on the near horizon, give us a reason to shout Hosanna! Praise the Lord!

When Worlds Collide
John 3.1-2, 20-32

Crossroads. The place where we make choices. The place where we make deals. The place where we change directions. Where things are joined or separated. Where things come together. Decisions are made. Fates are sealed.

This year, Jewish Passover and Easter overlap. Which is fitting, as the events of Holy Week and Resurrection Sunday are framed by Passover. The Passover meal, shared with family and close friends – those you love. This is where Jesus is on this night – with those he loved, sharing a Passover meal.

Passover recalls and commemorates a crossroads. Choices. The choices of Pharaoh and the choices of the sons and daughters of Israel.

Indiana Jones and the Last Crusade – remember that scene where they had to choose the actual Holy Grail from all the chalices on the table? The knight advises them to choose wisely. The bad guy – he chose…. unwisely. Pharaoh, even after plagues, warnings, and good advice, chose…. unwisely. And because of that choice, the first-born sons of Egypt did not survive the night. There's no do overs at a crossroads. You can backtrack and change direction, but you can never get back that original opportunity to choose wisely.

Discipleship – following Christ – happens at the crossroads. In the intersections. When worlds collide. The Passover meal shared by Jesus and his friends was the place where two worlds collided. The world that was – the brutality of the Roman Empire and the oppression of the people – and the world to come – the beloved community of God, where violence, and fear, and tears are no more. That collision came at the hands of one of Jesus' friends – the man whose very name has come to mean betrayal of the worst kind.

We read this story – and John goes to great trouble to make sure we have the benefit of hindsight so we know Judas was the…Judas in this story – and we probably think to ourselves "How can a person do that to someone they had followed on a trek full of ups and downs, sermons and mountains, boats and storms, healings and exorcisms? How could Judas have made such a bad choice?"

For indeed, he did choose…. Unwisely.

At this crossroads of a story, Jesus and his friends are together, celebrating Passover – a gentle, quiet dinner that has its roots in oppression and brutality. But also, one that celebrates the covenant of God with God's people. That night Jesus made clear – again – that he had no intention of throwing off the chains of Rome. And Judas made a choice. At the crossroads of the Kingdom of God and Empire of Rome, Judas made a choice.

Judas soon figured out that he'd chosen unwisely, thrown his support to the wrong kingdom, but there was nothing to do at that point. He made his choice blinded to the reality of God's glory in Christ. He thought he could see where things were headed, and he couldn't live with the choice, because it looked like failure. And so, he chose unwisely. That's the tricky thing about choices – sometimes the right choice looks so, so wrong while the wrong choice looks so, so right.

Discipleship happens in the crossroads. In the places where there are choices to make, stands to take. In the places where things change.

We would never betray a friend, much less Jesus, right? But the problem with a crossroads is that you have choices, but you don't always know where the choices lead. A crossroads can lure us into thinking that we can see where the road is going, but in my experience, you can only count on that in Ohio where everything is laid out in townships on a flat grid. But here, the turn toward the east may be just one s-curve away from heading south. Or even west. That's more like the way life works. We don't know that out of twelve unenlightened followers that we won't be the one that makes the choice that changes everything. That betrays a friend. Breaks a heart.

After Judas makes his choice, Jesus talks to his friends and tells them to stay alert for the next things God is doing. But the end of this chapter makes it clear that they don't understand. Peter is the apostle for whom the face palm was invented. He is forever making pronouncements he couldn't back up - about his loyalty, his desire to be the very best follower of Christ. But in that upper room that night, it wasn't Peter that needed to make a choice. Peter had not yet come to a crossroads. We don't yet know that Peter didn't do so well when he had to decide. And he would have loved a do over.

Discipleship happens in the crossroads. And sometimes we find ourselves in dire need of a do over. Wanting to turn back time. Finding ourselves, like Judas, bitterly repenting our choices that turned out to lead somewhere other than the road to Jesus. But grace happens too.

John wants to be sure we know that Jesus knew that Judas was the villain in this story – yet he was welcomed at dinner just like the others. John also wants us to know that Jesus knows that despite Peter's claims to never betray Jesus, when he comes to the crossroads, Peter will choose unwisely. But Jesus doesn't call him out. Peter is also welcomed at dinner; his feet are washed. Both Judas and Peter are still counted among those Jesus graced with love and kindness.

THAT is the ultimate good news – our choices don't affect our standing as children of God who come to Christ's table. We all a covered by grace – those of us who choose wisely, those who choose unwisely, those who do it right and those of us in constant need of do overs. None of us loved more, none of us loved less.

And because of Christ, we no longer need do overs. Because Christ makes a way when there is no way. Welcomes us when all we want to do is slink away. Loves us regardless of our choices – and tells us to love others the same way.

On a night where there was much to fear, when there was too little time and way too much left undone, Jesus welcomed his friends to a table of love and peace. And told them to go and do likewise.

Grace happens at the crossroads and enables our discipleship. Wherever we are, whatever our choices, God will welcome us at the table of grace and kindness.

Breathe In, Breathe Out

John 20. 19-31

The Sunday after Easter is usually called Low Sunday because after the pew packing events of Resurrection Sunday, finding a parking and sitting place is much easier that next week. And let's face it – after all that preparation – get the sanctuary ready, all those lilies, choir anthems – we're all tired.

So low expectations for this Sunday.

And then the lectionary throws this text out – the story we often call The Story of Doubting Thomas.

But seriously, who among us wouldn't be skeptical about the possibility of someone we loved who we had watched be arrested and killed, coming back for dinner? This story is custom written for the folks who intended to be here on Easter Sunday but missed it by Just. This. Much. Thomas missed Easter – and I suspect that his declaration of needing to see and touch the wounds may have been as much about Thomas trying to be cool in front of his friends as anything.

Because when the time comes Thomas doesn't have to touch Jesus to know it's for real. All it took was the reality of Jesus offering himself to Thomas, and Thomas knew for sure this was his friend, his teacher, his Lord, his God.

But the key point of this passage might be in the first words Jesus said in that room: Peace be with you.

In this passage, Jesus says that phrase three times – twice when he first appears with the disciples, and once the second time he shows up. And note this: Jesus breathed on them and said receive the Holy Spirit.

We're still a few weeks away from Pentecost, but in John's gospel, this is the coming of the Holy Spirit. The Spirit which, in the earthly absence of Jesus, will be the presence of God among them, to remind them of all the things he taught them, showed them. It's a very different scene than Luke paints in Acts There are no tongues of fire, no rushing wind – just the breath of Jesus, the same breath that blessed them with peace. The same breath that offered himself to Thomas – unafraid to face the one that expressed doubt in the face of mystery.

We often think epiphany must be accompanied by special effects and a killer soundtrack. The Holy Spirit arrives with a wind shear and fireworks. We think faith must be unshakable – there is no room for doubt in the heart of a believer.

But the words of Jesus remind us that sometimes, the presence of God shows up quietly, blessing us with peace – peace of mind, peace of spirit, peace of surroundings, peace of… well, just peace. We often expect God to show up with sound effects and soundtracks, but God usually shows up without the wrath and the judgement, and instead comes with peace and love. And understanding.

We don't get much peace in the current world, and there wasn't much peace in the world in which Jesus and Thomas lived. Or the one our parents, grandparents, great grandparents, or our ancestors of multiple generations ago lived in. If it's not the goths sacking Rome, it's the Huns crossing the Ural mountains; the black death taking out one out of every three people; the Crimean war – or any of the wars that were supposed to end all wars; smallpox, typhoid, polio, cholera, AIDS – any disease that strikes fear into our hearts; nuclear weapons, chemical weapons, the Gatling gun. There has never been a time or place since the earliest days of humans banding together in what we ironically call civilization that we haven't been able to create or stumble on to new and efficient ways of doing one another in and striking fear in to the hearts of one another. We don't usually greet one another with "peace be with you."

Our end-of-the-day blessing is often: are your doors locked and your phone close by?

But Jesus appeared to his disciples with the words "peace be with you" – and his last words for and to his followers were not a list of instructions for keeping the message alive. They were about love for one another. And peace. To go teach and preach. To go and do as he did – offer up self to others in spite of their doubt, or posturing, or just plain unwillingness to do the right thing.

Because God – through Jesus and the Holy Spirit speaks peace. Breathes peace. And breaths on us with peace.

This does not often go well in our current culture. We are not a people accustomed to being blessed with peace – we see it as something unattainable, even worthy of a good ironic laugh: because all we want is world peace. Sandra Bullock supplied the hand motions and fake tears, and we all got the joke. Because really, who wants world peace? It sounds good until you started thinking about the practicalities of the thing: it might involve black helicopters, unpaid loans to poorer countries, and the loss of national identity, right?

But that aside, God does come breathing peace, as much as we'd like to have God come in wrath and judgement, confirming that we are right, and those other folks are wrong.

Going back to the original doubter, Thomas, Jesus didn't beat him into submission with cherry picked verses of scripture. He simply offered himself, body and spirit, to Thomas, much as he offered himself up to the Romans. And while an attempt to convince Thomas might have led to Thomas having to dig in and protect his position, Jesus gave Thomas the opportunity to peacefully come to him.

On this low Sunday, when there is more space in the pews than there was last week, and when the lilies are looking not quite as grand as last week – it's easy to forget that there are 50 days in the season of Easter. And every week, the fading lilies will remind us that we are further and further out from the miracle of Resurrection Sunday. But the message hasn't changed, and the reality is this: Jesus didn't rise so that we could have a convincing argument to re-fill all the pews. The reality of Jesus' resurrection is grounded in peace and self-offering. And those are harder for us to take than a good, convincing argument with plenty of evidence.

Presbyterians in general have had a hard time with the idea of evangelism, because for far too long it's meant pulling someone aside and telling them what they are doing wrong. But what if, instead of starting out with a question that puts people on the spot – like "do you know Jesus?" – instead evangelism is reaching out, talking about Jesus and started the way Jesus did: peace be with you.

The action of passing the peace has started some good old-fashioned church fights. If you're not familiar with the idea, after the prayer of confession, after the assurance of pardon, the good church folk are given the opportunity to "greet one another with signs of peace."

People either love passing the peace, or they hate it. To make it easier for more people, lots of churches have watered it down into - "greet each other" and it becomes a mini social hour in the middle of worship. But I happen to love passing the peace. It's where the rubber hits the road for followers of Jesus.

Can you look at someone you don't particularly like and say, "the peace of Christ be with you?" Or your squirmy kid and say peace, rather than – stop that. Can you meet your boss on Monday morning with a breathing in of peace and a breathing out of faith? Can a republican and a democrat offer each other the peace of the Lord? Can they each breath in the presence of Jesus?

In this room, on Sunday morning, passing the peace of Christ ought to be easier than it is in any other place – because like the upper room where the disciples were hiding out, this is the most likely place for Jesus to be. The self-offering Jesus, as well as John the evangelist, reminds us that while Jesus' earthly presence was ending, the presence of God in the Holy Spirit would never end, would always be present.

And the message is what it always was: peace be with you.

John ends this passage with these words: Jesus did a bunch of other stuff, but I'm writing this down, so you can know the truth and believe, and by believing, have life in his name. Life here and now, full of peace.

John ends his gospel with the exchange between Jesus and his disciples that includes this: do you love me? Tend my sheep. Feed my sheep. Sheep, I believe are easily disturbed, frightened. Part of the work of the shepherd is to keep the sheep from stampeding in fear. (Insert hilarious mental image of stampeding sheep here)

What keeps us from stampeding in fear, going out half blind to reality from our fears and anxiety? Peace. May it be with you.

The peace of our Lord Jesus Christ be with you….

A Higher Law

Acts 11.1-18; John 13.31-35

It has been another one of those weeks. A week with news that seemed to catch folks by real surprise – like the new face of the $20 bill – and news that made the world tilt a bit – like the death of his royal purpleness, Prince. We're locked into what feels like a made up presidential election season – I've been watching reruns of West Wing at night while eating ice cream out of the carton to keep up my political denial. We all need coping skills. This weekend, part of my coping included hearing over and over the words of the artist who was, is and will be known as Prince:

Dearly beloved, we are gathered here together today to get through this thing called life.

And indeed, we are. But too often it seems like for every step we take forward, something yanks us back another three. If only this were a new development. But alas – this has been going on since the Garden, and the church is no stranger to it, either.

In what might be called the first contentious presbytery meeting, Peter has been hauled in front of other church leaders. Seems he has some 'splainin' to do. You see, he had met with, eaten with, and baptized this guy Cornelius, along with all of Cornelius' family. And Cornelius, you see, wasn't "one of them." He was, first, a Roman. A Gentile. And at this point in the church's history, all the followers of Jesus, were, first and foremost, Jewish. So, Cornelius **really** wasn't "one of them."

Oddly, what got Peter into hot water wasn't that he baptized Cornelius and company. It was that he ATE with them. Shared a meal. Table fellowship. Sat at table with… **them**. Who are not **us**.

How soon we forget.

Forget that Jesus, who at this point hadn't been gone from earth all that long, spent most of his meals out with sinners, drunkards, prostitutes, tax collectors, and other rogues, misfits and heathens. It is so, so easy to fall into the trap of "us" and "them." And "us" has got to be protected at all costs. "Us" is responsible making sure there is no danger to "our way of life."

And so, just a short time after the death and resurrection of Jesus, we have the very first church council. There were others over the 2000-year history of the church – most of which made clear what it is that Christians believe and do – but this was likely the first time the church had to figure out what came next.

Up until now, followers of Jesus Christ were basically part of the Jewish religious tradition. Even Paul, when he went to a new city, first found the synagogue to worship and teach. Christianity started as a Jewish sect, but as the good news spread, more people wanted in. For followers of Jesus in Jerusalem and surrounding areas, the answer was clear – if you want to be a follower of Christ, you must first be a Jew.

But then, here's Peter who has baptized an entire family of gentiles – without first requiring them to convert. True, what the folks in Jerusalem were most upset about was the fact that Peter had eaten at the same table as the gentiles. But maybe not so oddly – there's a power in sharing a meal. But then again, there's probably a sermon in there somewhere about what we tend to treat as the primary issue when we're thinking about how to spread the good news.

But back to today's point: Peter's explanation to the church council gathered there is to tell them a story. A story of a vision he had.

It was Passover weekend for Jewish communities this weekend, which means Seder meals were prepared and served all over the world last night. Dietary restrictions for kosher meals are much like they were laid out in Leviticus – certain animals were not to be eaten.

Peter's vision was of all these forbidden animals being lowered down to him, with a voice from heaven telling him to **Eat**.

But Peter's no fool – he's read the story of Adam and Eve. He's not falling for that so quickly.

The real-time version of this vision is told in the previous chapter of Acts – and Peter's recounting for the council at Jerusalem is nearly identical. Writing was hard in the first century – so if something is repeated, it's worth paying attention to. There's something important here to notice.

On one side of this conversation, we have the leaders of the church, concerned about preserving the peace, unity, and purity of the church. And that's important. Today, ordination vows for elders and ministers include a promise to preserve those things. So, having a set of rules or guidelines isn't an all bad thing. Presbyterians believe all things related to being church should be done decently and in order. We have a constitution; we have a book of **ORDER**, of all things. And a hefty portion of that book is related to protecting peace, unity, and purity of the church. As keepers of the body of Christ, we are tasked with making sure that toxic, destructive, and divisive elements don't damage the body.

It's easy, with the luxury of 2000 years of hindsight, to make this a case of white hats and black hats, with Peter decidedly wearing the white hat. But it's not that simple. With the luxury of hindsight, we can see that in this situation, there would either be two winners or two losers. This is not a zero-sum game. Some of those church leaders in Jerusalem may have been with Peter and Jesus in that upper room on the night of Jesus' arrest. They had been entrusted with a great truth – a truth that the apostle Paul says we hold in clay jars. Fragile containers. So, we shouldn't be too hasty in naming the Jerusalem church as bad guys.

On the other side stands Peter, who has had a vision which will expand the church, open the way for Paul to move throughout Asia

Minor and basically create most of the doctrine the church will still be following 2000 years later.

If Peter had not been able to make the church leaders see and believe what he'd seen and believed, it's possible that the movement that spread throughout the world and changed so much, might never have gotten out of that small area around the Sea of Galilee. There would have been no church for which to preserve the peace, unity, and purity.

As a spoiler, this wasn't the last time this subject was raised. Paul was called to Jerusalem to do the same kind of "splainin'. The church in Galatia had some helpful folks come to town and tell them they all needed to be good Jews before they could be good Christians. So, the preservation of the church was and is important – we should take it seriously. But we should also remember Peter's question: who am I that I can hinder God?

Who am I – who are we – that we can hinder God?

Our second passage today comes from the gospel of John. On the night of his arrest Jesus was sharing a Passover meal with his friends. All of them. Even the one he knew would betray him to his death. The one that would betray him and run away. The ones that would not be there to bear witness to his death. All of them were greeted with an act of love and humility – the washing of their feet. All of them shared in the meal.

If you knew you only had a short time, what would you say to your friends and family? These friends had followed him almost from the beginning. They'd heard what he had to say; witnessed the things he did; were often mystified at the people he chose for dinner companions. So, Jesus knew what he said here needed to be for them. And he gave them this: Love one another. Love each other the way I love you. Spread this – because this is how people will know you follow me: your love for one another.

Prince had some song lyrics that were deep, spiritual, and moving. But there's another band I want to quote this morning: U2. "Love is a higher law." This is what Jesus' last words were. "We have to carry each other."

In the weeks between Easter and Pentecost, the lectionary passages focus on the formation of the church – Christ's body on earth. Sometimes you wonder how passages got put together – but I understand why these are together. Preservation of the church is important – but love is the higher law. Protection of what we know is important – but love IS a higher law. The way we've always done things is important – but love is a higher law. We need institutions to create and maintain order – but love will always be the higher law. We don't know where God may lead us next. But here's something I can pretty much guarantee – it will probably challenge us in some way. Challenge us to remember that love is always the higher law – above Levitical dietary laws, above the books that maintain our order, above the way things have been – even above the way things are.

Most of the New Testament, in one way or another, wants us to remember who we are – beloved children of God. Little children – remember who you are, and how you are to show that. For they will know we are Christians by our love. May it ever be so.

A Mighty Wind

Acts 2.1-21

For the last seven weeks, since Easter, the lectionary passages have dealt with the establishment of the Church. Today, Pentecost Sunday, we celebrate the gift of the Holy Spirit, the comforter. The mighty wind of God.

And the lectionary pairs this story from Acts with the story in Genesis of the tower of Babel. In that story, everyone spoke the same language – and God gave them different languages so that they could not understand one another. On Pentecost, there are still different languages, but all can communicate because God supplied the translation services.

It's not hard to draw the parallels in that story – one a breaking apart, one a reconciliation. But there are lots of things going on in these passages.

The builders of the city and tower weren't necessarily all bad, are they? They wanted to make a name for themselves by building that city. In the building of the city and tower, they would celebrate what they had been able to do – all on their own. They would be safe within the walls of the city, would be able to protect themselves by having lookouts in the tower. Their fear is that they would be scattered all over the world if they didn't do something to ensure and protect their future and way of life. Scattered out into a world full of much to fear. We get that, right? That need to protect ourselves and those people and things we love is something we can understand.

The disciples and other followers of Jesus, would have understood that need for protection and closeness. They were huddled together in a locked room, afraid of being found, perhaps. And suddenly they were sent out of that room – and I suspect – **VERY** surprised to find that they were suddenly multi-lingual. And from that place, those followers would eventually be scattered around the world – a world still full of scary things, but these were not the same scared disciples that had deserted Jesus at Calvary. From this point on, the disciples seemed to understand better who Jesus was, and what their calling was to be.

Two stories. Two sets of folks scattered out. In the first story, they people wanted to make a name for themselves. In Acts, they had a name, and were empowered to preach in that name – fearlessly, as it turns out. Fearless despite their fear…

And something to note – in chapter 1, Luke tells us that those gathered believers numbered about 120, and some of them were women. And when the spirit came, it came to all of them, and all of them were given the ability to speak in other languages. Some of those little details like that have been overlooked – and I want to make sure women and girls know they aren't off the hook to follow the call of Christ wherever it might lead.

But I digress.

We live in a world that has much to fear. And if you don't have anything to be afraid of, watch tv for a couple of hours. Even better, watch tv during the month of October. Political campaigns will do a really good job of telling you what to fear. And who to fear. Our natural inclination is to wall ourselves in, make sure that who and what we are collectively – and individually – is safe. Secure. Vote for the person most likely to provide safety and security for US. To mitigate our fears.

But then that pesky Holy Spirit comes along. And Paul, writing to the church in Rome, says we did not get this spirit to be afraid. Instead, we have a spirit of adoption. Those led by the spirit of God are children of God. Fear not – and so on.

Pentecost took place during one of the busiest weekends in Jerusalem. The city was full of visitors from different places. All these other people and languages – Parthians, Medes, Elamites,

Libya, Rome, Cretans, Arabs – the disciples were speaking all these languages. Lots of diversity.

That crowd in Jerusalem on that first Pentecost certainly **was** diverse. And they were united by their skepticism of the disciples. But despite all the differences, the many languages, this passage tells us that all of us are the same in God's view. Peter began to quote the prophet Joel – a prophet who preached to the scattered tribes of Israel – as if the original words were given to more than just the children of Israel. Peter, through the power of the spirit – delivered the words of the prophet to everyone there, regardless of where they came from.

And it's radical stuff, really. In a time and place where only grown men "mattered," Peter tells the gathered that their DAUGHTERS would prophesy, the YOUNG men would see visions. Gender, age, first language, slave or free – all those distinctions of humanity – no longer matter. When the Spirit blows through, things change. Human constructs get swept away, and we are all equal in the sight of God. And yet we retain our individual selves – another one of those paradox of faith. Unity in our diversity. We are one not because of a common language, world view, doctrinal belief, skin color, or any of the other things we think can separate us. Or want to separate us. We are one because God makes us one.

Unity – the real kind, that includes and embraces our differences – is scary and hard. It's easier to build a city to protect us and to believe that once we've done that, we are protected. But the call of God, through the power of the spirit is not to homogenous sameness but to participate in the miracle of unity through difference. "We are one in the spirit, we are one in the Lord."

The Spirit comes to knock down the walls that separate us, flatten the towers that let us determine what might be threatening. The spirit sends us out and into scary places, among people and things we might not choose to be among, were it left up to us.

But never without equipping us. Never alone.

The spirit equips us to live in a spirit of community, covenant, of mutual commitment with one another and with God. The power of God, manifested in this mighty wind that blows through our notions of what we have in common and replaces them with the only thing we truly have in common: we are called and led by the Spirit of God. No matter our differences – or our sameness, for that matter – we are still called by God to live in such a way that our differences become at the same time, both more and less important.

In the first century, the father of the family – the patriarch – is the one responsible for making sure that everyone else has what they need. If you're part of the family, you are under the protection of the patriarch.

We have such protection, such provision from God. The God we call "Father."

Part of what got Jesus crossways of the religious and political leaders of his day was his familiarity with God among people who never spoke the name of God – only referred to the Holy One or used an anagram. But Jesus dared call God "father." And with Pentecost, we are gifted with that same level of familiarity – a word which indicates that we are "family."

Unlike the builders of that great city and tower of Babel, we don't have to make a name for ourselves – it's been done for us. Adopted into the family of God, heirs of the promise, led by the spirit. Given visions and dreams to take out into the world with the message of good news.

And as we go, one in the spirit, the world will know who we are – whose we are; they will know we are Christians how? By our love. And that's a good news message the world wants to hear....

Freedom: Not Just Another Word
Galatians 5.1, 13-25; Luke 9.51-62

I love my satellite radio. Just the other day, I heard one of my favorite songs – Janis Joplin, singing "Me and Bobby McGee." That Kris Kristofferson, he knows how to write a song. And he's a man who knows about freedom, and how sometimes freedom isn't all it's cracked up to be. It is, to quote, "just another word for nothing left to lose."

And the more I thought about it this week, an awful lot of the music I like, apparently, has something to do with being free, not being free, talking, thinking, singing about freedom. I started a play list, in fact.

But back to Bobby McGee - most of the time, I don't think we think of freedom as nothing left to lose. Instead, we think of freedom as the ability to do whatever we want.

I saw this cartoon of a teenager thinking that when he grew up, he was going to stay up late, run with scissors, not wear a seat belt, swim less than 30 minutes after eating… you know – all those things that kids don't get to do when they're kids. Freedom. Getting to do whatever we want.

The real irony is that when you are finally old enough to have that kind of freedom, you usually don't do them – because you know it isn't in your best interest to run with scissors. Or that the cost of a ticket for not wearing a seat belt isn't worth the effort. Staying up late makes it hard to get to work on time…and you don't exactly have to work, but it helps if you have money when you go to the grocery or the gas station. It's been interesting to watch my son go from a teenager who can't wait to be old to do what he wants, to lament that he can't do what he wants unless he works – which is so NOT what he wants to be doing….

The reality is that the freedom that children imagine adults have is really not freedom at all. And this is what Paul wants the church in Galatia to know.

Freedom isn't being able to do whatever you want. Freedom is the ability to choose whatever you do and how you do it.

Slavery, on the other hand, is the antithesis of freedom – and Paul knew the Galatians would understand slavery. The Roman Empire, as part of their conquest, brought slaves back to the territories, including Asia Minor, where Galatia was located. They would march them into the city, wearing a wooden yoke that had two purposes – to keep the slave from being able to easily escape, and to announce to the world that this person was no longer a person, but was property. The Romans used wooden yokes; in this country, shackles on slaves – and on prisoners – mark someone who has lost their freedom; the Germans used tattoos on the arms of death camp prisoners – and all of these things are designed to take away someone's dignity and personhood and make clear that the this is no longer a person, but property. For them, freedom no longer exists.
But we are not just enslaved by others – we can also enslave ourselves. On my playlist is an Eagles' song "Take It Easy: "so often it happens, that we live our lives in chains… and we never even know we have the key…."

We are so used to being enslaved, that we've lost the ability to understand freedom – or even want it. And Paul warned the Galatians this could happen to them. You've tasted the freedom of being released from the law, the freedom that comes from the grace and mercy of God. Why would you want to go back to that?

We are called to freedom – and that's certainly not having nothing to lose. Freedom – much as I love Kris Kristofferson – is really having everything to lose.

Freedom in Christ – this freedom is not about doing what we want but being able to be who we are intended to be. Like children, we often think of freedom and free will in terms of being able to do what we please. But Paul warns the Galatians – and us – that to think that way is dangerous. Freedom in Christ is freedom to be new creatures in Christ, released from the chains of this life. Paul uses "flesh" to describe a life that is concerned only with ourselves and our wants. This is self-indulgence – and listen to what it produces:

Fornication, impurity, licentiousness, idolatry, sorcery, enmities, strife, jealousy, anger, quarrels, dissensions, factions, envy, drunkenness, carousing, and things like these. Everything on this list has its root in self-indulgence, concerned with what we want, how we feel. And none of these things puts anything positive back into the world – or into us.

On the other hand, the fruits of the spirit – a life lived knowing that true freedom is not self-indulgence – are: love, joy, peace, patience, kindness, generosity, faithfulness, gentleness and self-control. Everything on this list has to do with moving beyond our own wants and needs. Everything on that first list – these are the things that will not be present in the promised kingdom of God. That second list – that's the very foundation for the promised kingdom. Those are the things that last, the things that Jesus taught – and that the Spirit gives us. The freedom that we have in Christ is not to indulge ourselves – but to become a new creature. Freedom **from** the human nature to think only of ourselves and freedom **to** love others – both as God loves other and as God commanded us to love others.

To try and exchange this freedom **from** ourselves with a freedom **for** our self is to die spiritually, says Paul. It replaces the sacrifice of Christ with the idol of free will. Seeking God any way other than through grace cuts us off from grace. Seeking freedom to do anything other than the will of God enslaves us – even if we don't recognize it. Because then we – and our world – is limited to what we can imagine, what we can accomplish, what we can see with our eyes and experience.

"So often it happens – that we live our lives in chains, and we never even know we have the key...."

We don't know we're enslaved. In the gospel passage this morning, the disciples haven't yet given up the freedom to see the world only through their own experience. They go ahead of Jesus into Samaria to prepare things, but they get no welcome, because Jesus is headed to Jerusalem. There's a history here –the Samaritans and the Jews didn't get along, and it's all because of methods of worship. So, because Jesus was headed into Jerusalem for Passover, rather than up the mountain to celebrate it the way the Samaritans thought they should, the disciples didn't get the kind of welcome they thought they deserved.

There's an interesting side track we could take here about freedom of worship, freedom of religion. Or the history of conflict in that region and how it's pretty much been religious from the start. We are so enslaved to our ways of being God's people, that we often aren't able to be God's people. That's a sermon for another day – but don't lose that thought.

The disciples offer to bring down fire from heaven to destroy the Samaritans because they dissed Jesus. Can't you just see Jesus sort of shaking his head? We'd never be that way, right?

Anyway, as they go along, they pick up more followers, including one Jesus believes isn't ready to give up his comforts to follow. The journey with God isn't necessarily TO somewhere, especially to somewhere with air conditioning and 300 thread count sheets. Another **wants** to follow but needs to bury his father – or to put it another way, needs to wait until his father dies and he has the family money, so he can either buy the ac and the 300 thread count sheets, or maybe be the most powerful person in Jesus' organization – the one able to call the shots. Another wants to say goodbye to all those back home – maybe thinking he'll get a wonderfully emotional good-bye party and a hefty collection of farewell cards full of cash. Does any of this sound familiar? I'll be happy to be more involved – but on my terms... Happy to come along, but first I must do these other things that are more important.

These potential followers of Jesus are enslaved to their own way of seeing things. To their own wants and needs. They never even know the key to what enslaves them is right in front of them. Just like them, we want – we NEED – our journey with Christ to be based in our own needs and wants. We are enslaved – but Paul reminds us that this is the case only because we allow it to be.

But wait, there's more. The grace and freedom of God frees us not only from our own needs and wants – it also frees us from our past mistakes. Frees us from guilt over the huge errors in judgment. Frees us from remorse from the bad choices. Frees us having to second guess ourselves. Frees us from fear about what comes next. Frees us from our inability to believe that we deserve to be loved. (That's the one where we often get tripped up.)

There's been a soundtrack to this sermon. At this point, the horns swell up behind Aretha Franklin as she sings freedom.... freedom.... freedom....

The Supremes beg – set me free, why doncha?

Bob Dylan sings the Chimes of Freedom flashing.... (apparently, I know no music recorded after 1975....)

But there **should** be a soundtrack for this... We should be singing about freedom with huge horn sections and flashy beaded gowns and good bands in full houses. Because **this** is the good news, friends – we have been freed from the slavery that requires us to account and justify. We have been released into the realm of grace – it makes no sense for us to continue in those self-indulgent, selfish ways of being and seeing. We've been called.

The question this morning is this: Are you hoping for a call to comfort? Are you hoping to answer the call as the one with the power to call the shots? Are you hoping for an outpouring of love and support from those around you?

Or – are you willing to celebrate this freedom by loving people the way God loves people? To quote the prophet Aretha – you better think.

This freedom is less glitzy. Less comfortable. Less about us. In fact - nothing about us. But it's this freedom that empowers us to follow the new commandment that Jesus gave his disciples as they shared bread and wine – love one another. Love one another. And that calls for a whole new soundtrack....

Great Expectations
Mark 6.1-13

Expectations can be a funny thing – they can drive us on to greater things or cripple us and hold us back. It's a rare person who is totally immune to the expectations of others – and generally we call those people sociopaths...

It's our expectations that allow us to be surprised – in good ways and bad ways – allow us to be disappointed, to give affirmation, to withhold affirmation.... In human interactions, we are bound up in our own and others' expectations. And sometimes, those things collide. Mark gives us a look into a moment when Jesus' humanity is on full display, along with the humanity of others. I don't know about you, but I tend forget that in addition to being divine, Jesus was also fully human. The same man who taught that the meek will inherit, the mourners will dance, the last will be first – this same man was righteously indignant enough to turn over tables in the temple – and he was apparently a bit indignant here as well.

But the gospel – the good news – contains the story of humans learning the ways of God, and let's face it, we're not that good at it. We must keep learning and learning. And we don't always appreciate the lessons.

This weekend we celebrate our declaration of independence from what was perceived as an oppressive empire, after a very short period where change happened very fast – to the delight of some, and the devastation of others. Some celebrate, some don't – which is the messy truth of democracy. One person's victory is another's crushing defeat. And we tend to define our lives in this kind of zero sum reality – if one wins, another must lose. There is only so much truth – and if I have it, you obviously don't. On some level we know that's not the case, but our default is never to think in terms of I'm right, but you're right too. And if we did, our entire political, economic, and social framework would collapse. Our default expectations define our reality – the unexpected, the unexplained can force our reality to shift, and that is not comfortable.

It's our expectations that fuel our overall reality. We expect things to even out, for there to be winners and losers, ying and yang, this and that, us and them. And in the case of Jesus and the disciples, they have been the winners so far. In the last few weeks, Mark has related stories of Jesus healing the sick, calming the storm, teaching and preaching – and generally getting good reviews. This trip to Nazareth should have been a victory lap – back home, fully expecting that the stories of their exploits would have preceded them. The winning should have continued.

And Jesus was totally ON. Brought his A game to the teaching in the synagogue. And at first, everything was going great. Then, folks remembered who he was. Little Jesus, Joseph and Mary's son. The boy that helped his father out in the carpenter's shop. How could THIS person presume to have a prophetic voice? How could HE teach them the meaning of the holy writings? And because Jesus did not conform to their expectations, their anxiety was tripped, and they went into default mode. Because this is Jesus who is only a carpenter's son, he can't have gotten this wisdom legitimately. And before you know it they are reexamining the truth they have heard and rather than the truth shifting their expectations, they allowed their expectations to shift the truth. They simply couldn't imagine the hometown kid as a prophetic teacher.

But, Jesus had a habit of not conforming to expectations.

This is where we often run into trouble. Jesus refuses to fit into our notion of what a savior should be. We want the kingdom to come, we want Jesus to teach us, to lead us, but like the people of Nazareth, I suspect that we want Jesus to teach us things we already know. Or things we don't know but don't challenge what we know. Or think. Or do. We want Jesus to affirm our beliefs and justify our actions. And Jesus remains amazed at our unbelief.

The thing that's always surprising to me is that the people who should know Jesus best – all through the gospels – seem to be oblivious to who and what Jesus is. And I'm not sure that's changed so much in 2000 years. You'd think that at some point humans would get smarter about stuff, but apparently, we are a stubborn people.

I have no idea on what Jesus preached that morning. I suspect it was a version of the sermon on the mount – the mourners will dance, the meek will inherit, the first will be last, the mighty brought low. When we hear this, we initially think – yeah, that's some good stuff. But then we think – that's not the way the world works. All that's true – but it's not **really** true, right?

Strangers knew there was something special about Jesus - they followed him to hear him teach, watch him heal the sick, do amazing things. But the people closest to him – those who watched him grow up – strong in the lord, the scripture tells us – were so surprised by him they were angry, which is often the default response to surprise.

Just as an aside – if you haven't seen Inside Out, the Pixar movie – go. I was going to base my whole sermon on that movie but didn't want to spoil it if you haven't seen it yet. Just go. And take your teenagers. And here ends the commercial….

But surprise which expresses itself as anger is often the response to Jesus' message that the hungry should be fed, the poor should be helped, the powerful are not really the powerful, you should love other people more than you love yourself regardless of their worthiness – and Jesus remains amazed at our unbelief. The folks in the synagogue that morning heard the message, recognized the message as wise and prophetic and true, but in the end, missed the message. Missed the opportunity to really, really hear Jesus.

This happens a lot – the world is full of people who claim to be closer than close to Jesus, but I suspect they have missed the message. Or maybe they ignore the message, because the second half of the gospel lesson tells this truth: when we follow Jesus, we get sent out to places we might not choose to go, to interact with people we might not want to know and may have to leave behind the things that make us comfortable. And we might not get to choose our own traveling companions.

Jesus sent out the apostles – the very word means "one who is sent" – out to preach, teach, heal. Sent them with the bare minimum of belongings so they would have to depend on the kindness of others. Seriously, who'd do that – because, let's face it, people generally aren't that kind. And didn't tell them to beat people over the head with the message –if the message was rejected move on.

This is hard – this following Jesus this way. It's much, much easier to sit in our own place – like the folks in Nazareth that morning – and feel smug about our ability to tell the truth from not truth. And to share the truth from our seats of comfort.

The last couple of weeks there has been no shortage of people willing to sit in the seats of comfort and lob truth bombs over the walls. It's so easy to share the truth that way. We can share the truth about politics, economics, marriage, health care, you name it – and never have to leave the comfort of our own experience. The internet – and Facebook particularly – has made it so easy to pontificate on nearly anything that our ability to lob these truth bombs in multiple directions has never been so easy. Or faceless.

This is not how Jesus intended the truth to be shared, friends. Jesus sent folks out into the trenches with no cushion of comfort, no protection under the law, no guarantees of success. He sent them out. And in the end, they changed. And they changed the world. We can't change the world from the safe and comfortable environs of our own reality.

He sent out the apostles to tell the truth to people face to face – the same people on whose kindness they depended.

Think about that for a moment – how different would the truth sound if you knew the person hearing it was providing your next meal? Or was providing the roof over your head? If you lived out your faith depending on the kindness and good will of the people with whom you were sharing the truth? If our faith was rooted, nurtured, and sustained by an awareness of God's grace and the only appropriate response to that grace: gratitude. If we extended grace to others from a place of gratitude to God? If our message of truth and grace was clothed in gratitude and humility rather than the moral high ground?

When we hear the truth from Jesus, we have choices – we can react with anger born out of fear that this truth will force us to rearrange our reality. Or we can take that truth out into the world – not as a weapon to demand what we deserve, but as a gift that can come from no other place. This is the challenge this morning – to listen for the voice of Jesus, the truth of his message – and to decide: does that truth change our view of the world, or does our view of the world change that message? Jesus said all the law and prophets can be summed up in two sentences: Love the lord your God will all your heart, mind and soul. And love your neighbor as yourself. Jesus's challenge is to hear those words and let them change expectations, change reality, change the world.

And then to take those words out into the world, and to live those words in the world.

Are we the people in the synagogue in Nazareth? Or are we the sent people, taking the message of Jesus and the vision of the beloved kingdom of God into the world? As we go out from this place and into the world – may we indeed go INTO the world.

Simplicity, Interrupted

John 6.56-69

You know, when you sit down to write a sermon, one of the first things you do after you read through the passages, is to consult commentaries. Commentaries are written by people smarter than I am, and the people who write them have done a great deal of what a former employer of mine called "deep thinkin'." It's easy to get lost in the commentaries, reading them over and over. And over – forgetting that the inspiration for any sermon should be the text itself.

Then there's that whole issue of the title. I stalled if I could, because without fail, once I title a sermon, it's a foregone conclusion that the sermon will end up having nothing to do with the title. One of my professors at seminary once suggested that if we were forced to title a sermon, we should keep it generic, something like "Grace – Still Amazing. But I went with "I Thought It was Supposed to Be Simple." That wasn't so much a sermon title as what I was saying over and over the day I needed a title. And it didn't work all that well.

I thought this was supposed to be simple. I took all those seminary courses, I made good grades, and I really learned a lot from all that reading and writing. I've written sermons before. So, sitting down to write a sermon shouldn't be all that difficult, should it?

I consider myself progressive in the use of technology – so I thought I could simplify what was becoming a complicated sermon writing process. I typed into the Google search window "I thought this was supposed to be simple" and got like 10 million hits or something ridiculous like that. Apparently, I am not the only one that finds things complicated that should be simple.

And after all that, here we are this morning, preparing to look at a passage from the gospel of John. It should be simple.

But these are hard words. Eating flesh and drinking blood – even if we think of this metaphorically, it is still hard. Each time we have communion we eat the broken body of Christ and drink the spilled blood of Christ – but on a spiritual level. We know that we are not eating actual flesh and drinking actual blood. We make the hard words a bit easier to digest.

But if those words are hard for us, think how hard it would have been to hear these words if you were in the congregation of the synagogue in Capernaum on that day. Under Levitical law, it was forbidden to even touch a corpse – how much worse would it be to think of eating flesh and drinking blood.

We know this was hard for them to hear – because the passage tells us the people said, "hey, this is hard". This is the crowd that has followed Jesus out to the place where they need to be fed, met Jesus as he stepped off the boat at Capernaum, and now has followed him to synagogue. These people have followed Jesus for quite some time, and up to now, it's been all healing, and casting out demons, and feeding of multitudes, and walking on water. One miracle after another. So, the crowd was expecting more of the same. It was supposed to be simple….

Then they hear these words of Jesus: "These are hard things." Way too hard. So, nearly everyone leaves at that point. Goes off to find something simpler. Easier to swallow – literally and figuratively, I suspect. When all was said and done, Jesus looked around and saw that a goodly number of those people that had been following him around, ending up at the weekly service at the synagogue, were gone. Vamoosed. Disappeared into the countryside. Off to find the simple life.

The new Revised Standard Version that we read this morning translates verse 60 as "who can accept it" – referring to the teaching of Jesus in the synagogue. But the NIV translates this verse a bit closer to the original Greek. In that translation, the question is – "who can listen to this?" The people who left the synagogue that morning couldn't even listen to the words Jesus was saying. They came for the miracles and the free lunch and they left when it just wasn't that simple.

I suspect that in churches all over the place this morning there are people sitting in church, convinced that it's all so simple. Worship requires only our presence, only our hearing, only our us-ness – God will do the rest, we think. Worship is such a simple thing.

But – and I'm sure by now you can see this coming – things are not always as simple as we think – or as we'd like.

I am the product of a Baptist preacher's family. My sister, who has gone to church all her life – probably more faithfully than I have – told me recently that she loves me, but she just can't enjoy a Presbyterian service. It's not the theology that bothers her – she's fine with that. It's the expectation that she needs to participate. According to her, we should all be thin and fit because of all the standing up and sitting down we do in a service. For her, a church service is more of a spectator sport. But it's just not that simple.

Worship requires us to hear things that sometimes we just can't stand to listen to. Requires us to acknowledge our smallness and God's greatness. Requires us to acknowledge that we are sinful creatures and ask for forgiveness. Requires us to give back something of what God has given to us. Requires us to stand and affirm our beliefs out loud.

Churches all over the place are full of empty spaces this morning where people have come looking for something simply and left when the teachings and the expectations were hard.

In my "day job," I sit in on lots of conversations about what to do about declining numbers in churches. What should be the strategies for bringing people into church. Should we change our services? Should we build better facilities? Offer more programming? In the passage we read this morning, Jesus didn't seem to be all that concerned with how many people were left after he finished talking. In fact, he offered the few that were left the opportunity to go as well.

And Peter – bless his heart – good ole Peter is always willing to speak up. Peter says to Jesus, "and where would we go?" In the other three gospels, Peter's words are recorded a bit differently. Matthew, Mark and Luke's gospels have Peter declaring that Jesus is the Christ, the Messiah – the one that has been sent. But in John, Peter calls Jesus the Holy One – the one that is the only place they can go, the way to God, the source of eternal life, what they have been looking for. Peter doesn't reassure Jesus that what he said was not all that hard – hearing about eating flesh and drinking blood would have been just as offensive to Peter as it was to the ones that left. But where else would they go?

When we come to this place, do we come with the expectation that we will leave here feeling better? That we will have been fed by the Spirit and given a week's worth of armor to protect us from what the world will throw at us?

Or do we come with a sense of awe and fear of shock, realizing that we are before the Holy One of God, who may say things we find difficult to listen to, much less accept. Do we come because we have no better place to be, or because we simply cannot be anywhere else?

Writer Annie Dillard, in her book *Teaching a Stone to Talk*, takes churchgoers to task for underestimating the power of real worship:

> Does anyone have the foggiest idea what sort of power we so blithely invoke? Or, as I suspect, does no one believe a word of it? The churches are children playing on the floor with their chemistry sets, mixing up a batch of TNT to kill a Sunday morning. It is madness to wear ladies' straw hats and velvet hats to church; we should all be wearing crash helmets. Ushers should issue life preservers and signal flares; they should lash us to our pews. For the sleeping god

may wake someday and take offense, or the waking god may draw us out to where we can never return." -Annie Dillard in *Teaching a Stone to Talk* (Harper Collins, 2009)

As we prepare to eat and drink in remembrance of what God has done for us, do we understand the implications of it? When we hear the words of institution, are they words we have heard hundreds of times, or are they words that send shivers down our spine. Do we hear them and get the warm fuzzies or do we squirm a bit in our seat? Is it easy to hear? Simple?

There is nothing simple in the act of worship, and we should not take either the privilege or the responsibility for granted. To come into the presence of God is an awesome privilege. To hear the word of God, to take part in the death and resurrection of Jesus, to invoke the Spirit of God – this brings an awesome responsibility. Most people can't handle it. They can't stick around.

But a few heard and realized what they were hearing.

And they stayed.

And this living God called them out to places they had never imagined, never dreamed of, never wanted. They had no idea that day in the synagogue how their lives would change, or end, but they knew this: they had found something they didn't even know they were looking for. Where else could they go?

We think it should be simple – come to church, confess our sins, go home, live a life of peace and quiet, doing good works here and there, living out a life of quiet faith, worshipping on Sunday to fuel that faith. But it's not that simple. When we come to worship, come to remember – we run the risk of changing everything if we truly encounter God.

We have come here to worship – are you willing to take that risk?

Come – now is the time to worship.

Strange Bedfellows

Matthew 22.5-22

As luck would have it, the great minds that put together the lectionary texts dropped this parable right into the beginning of stewardship season. Some years we get this parable, some years we get Zacchaeus, some years the parable of the talents. All at the time of year when we begin to talk seriously about money.

The budget committee and the session and trustees have approved a proposed budget – and you'll get a chance to see that before the annual congregational meeting in January, when you receive, of course, a letter about stewardship next month. That letter will talk about what we do with our money. And this parable gives me a great chance to talk about money, what we do with it, how we use it… But I'm going to pass on that chance this morning.

Because at the end of the day, I don't think this story isn't about money at all. It's about something completely different.

This is a story about strange bedfellows, and the enemy of my enemy being my friend.

Jesus, not to put too fine a point on it, is making a nuisance of himself. He's going around the area, going into the synagogues and teaching things that are very popular among the people, but not so popular with the religious leaders. Or the political leaders. People are following him, people are putting his name forth as the one that finally bring Israel back the glory it once had. Make it great again. And this was causing problems for two groups of people, who normally had nothing but loathing for each other: The Pharisees and the Herodians. One group represented the Jewish religious leadership, and one represented a group that believed the best avenue for Israel to thrive was to cooperate with the Romans.

Now – I bet you are already slotting the characters and situation into our modern political and geo political circumstances, right? You've decided who is who in this story and trying to fit the moral of the story into a specific policy, platform, whatever.

Which is exactly what the Pharisees and the Herodians were up to. Trying to fit the things of faith into a political, national, sociological paradigm. And like trying to fit a square peg into a round hole, the only way they could do that was to shave off the edges of the things of faith. And these two groups had done that – granted they had shaved off the corners differently, but the sharpness of faithfulness and relationship to God had taken a back seat to preserving the way things are – or even trying to accomplish the way things should be.

Because what happens when you try to put things of faith into a sociological or political kind of framework is that strange kinds of alliances seem to appear. Normally, the Pharisees and the Herodians would have nothing to do with one another. But Jesus is a threat to both groups – he's telling the people stories like the Good Samaritan, which flies in the face of Levitical law. Or stories like the wicked tenants – which could be interpreted as a threat to the delicate balance the Herodians sought with Rome. And so, we have these two groups, working together to try and trick Jesus into making a mistake that would get him arrested and off the street. Strange bedfellows indeed.

Here was their plan: there was a tax the Jews were required to pay, and it could only be paid with this kind of coin that had Caesar's face on it, and words that indicated the divinity of Caesar. Jews found this a particularly galling tax, because to pay it meant that they were complicit in saying Caesar was a god. And commandment number one was there is one God, and the Lord your God is it.

So, these two groups devised a trap: if Jesus said it was okay to pay the tax, then the Pharisees had him for violating the first commandment. If he said it wasn't okay to pay the tax, then the Herodians had him for treason. Either way, Jesus would be in jail, and they could go back to fighting each other rather than this problematic rabbi who was upending the apple cart.

And again, I bet your mind is already working this into a modern political kind of frame. But Jesus' reaction to this trap is important – not because of the "render unto Caesar" quote, but because he simply broke the framework in which the question was asked.

We remember the render unto Caesar part of Jesus' answer, but we don't often quote the rest of that sentence: and give back to God that which belongs to God.

Jesus's answer satisfied neither the Pharisees nor the Herodians. Rather than give the either/or answer, Jesus made clear that whose image is on the coin of the realm is secondary to the reality that humans are created in the image of God, and the image imprinted in and on us makes the questions of political strategy and power dynamics just so much noise.

As people of faith, I think we lose something important when we spend most of our time worrying about who is and who is not in power and inserting ourselves into political frameworks by telling ourselves that politics and religion are somehow connected.

When we focus on making politics and religion an either/or choice – and in this country, we have – you run the risk of losing the awareness that other humans are not "them" in opposition to "us." What the Pharisees and the Herodians had forgotten was that when you start talking about what belongs to whom, and whether we should be aligned with one side or another, when issues are boiled down to either/or, we tend to forget that 1) we belong to God; and b) we are supposed to be aligned with God.

We are to be aligned with God. Not the other way around.

We get that backwards all the time. We think God is on our side – which is true only when we start out on God's side. But that's a sermon for another time.

Everything we have, everything we are – it all comes from God. Not from economic security, not from trade agreements, not from all those things we tend to think are important in the long term. Those are things we work within – not things that define who we are.

We belong to God – created and imprinted with God's image, as is every human. That's our defining characteristic, that's where our loyalty lies, and that's what we tend to forget in all the noise of a world that forces us into either/or choices that have nothing to do with being a child of God.

Instead we decide what is right and wrong based on our politics, not on our relationship with God. We lift or condemn based not on Jesus' example of mercy and love, but on an imposed framework of if you are this, you cannot be that. We emphasis what makes us different and divides us rather than what connects and unites us.

And it's a trap – because it is far easier to define yourself by what you are not than by what you are. It's far easier to demonize the "other side" than it is to look squarely at others – and ourselves through the lens of love and mercy. I don't know about you, but every time I engage in a little introspection and find something I don't like about myself, the first thing I do is find something or someone that is worse. At least I'm not that. And it's not hard to find someone else worse than me.

We are to give to God what is God's – which is our whole self: heart, mind, soul. It's all God's. When we do that, everything else can fade into the background. What we do with our money, our possessions, our lives – that's important. But if we ask ourselves questions about how we use the gifts we are given without first determining what God would have us do, we are putting carts and horses in the wrong order.

Let us never forget that we belong to God, imprinted with God's image. And render unto God what is God's.

For All the Saints
Isaiah 25.6-9; Revelation 21.1-6a

After all the witches and warlocks and pirates and princesses and all the other awesomely dressed up candy-holics that came to our houses last night, we are gathered here this morning on the first of November. All saint's day. Traditionally, this is the day we honor those who have gone before. One of the mysteries of our faith is that we relate to believers – and saints – in every time and place, and on this day, we celebrate both that connection and that great cloud of witnesses....

So, I will admit to it – I am an internet news junkie. I've always been one of those people interested in news. I would read three newspapers a day, watch the local news every evening, national news. But these days, the news isn't what it used to be. For one thing, newspapers have cut their staff so much that nearly every newspaper in the nation prints pretty much the same news – and the notion of local news has changed so much over the past several years. In a world where "breaking news" covers everything from the beginning of a war to an accident clogging the freeway, news (as I like to say) pretty much isn't.

But old habits die hard, and I still like to keep up, but these days I do it almost exclusively on line. There are several websites I read several times a day, and the truth is, the same stuff is on every one of them. And I'm not sure that the latest nonsense by Jon Gosslin actually qualifies as news, but I'm still there reading it.

My willingness to accept whatever is put out there as "news" is not unique. I think as a country, we've pretty much not missed the "real news" – the kind that actually wanted us to think and form an opinion and actually welcome news that gives us our opinions fully formed. To really know what's going on in the world could be more than we would want to know – to quote Jack Nicholson in A Few Good Men – it could be that we can't **handle** the truth.

John of Patmos, in the book of Revelation, wasn't sugarcoating the truth for the people of the churches located in Asia Minor. He was writing to people who were living the truth of the Roman Empire – an empire that would tolerate no difference of opinion from theirs. The Romans told the people they conquered what the news was – opinions and all. And this was the news in a nutshell – the emperor was god, and everyone in the Roman Empire was to worship the emperor.

This caused a problem for Christians. If you didn't call attention to yourself, you were fine. But should that change, Christians were often threatened with death if they did not light incense in worship of the emperor. And in the time that John was writing, there were many people who would not perform he simple act of lighting incense and call the emperor God – and they were killed. And the Romans really knew some creative ways of killing.

Over the centuries of Christian history, there have always been those who were unwilling to compromise their faith in even small ways. These are among the saints that we celebrate on this All Saints Day – remembering those that have gone before us, some of them giving their own lives so that we might worship without fear of death, believe in the one true God who makes all things new.

I suspect we tend to avoid the book of Revelation, because the images are frightening… The end of the world is frightening stuff. But the overall message of Revelation is not the end of the world. The message of Revelation is the beginning of the new life. The redeemed world. The new world.

The kingdom come – come down to earth. This is the true hope, the true promise of God to the children of God. In this morning's scripture, we have two descriptions of the kingdom come – one from Isaiah and one from Revelation – and they are remarkably similar. In fact, John, in writing Revelation referred to the Isaiah passage. His audience would have probably been very familiar with that passage.

The world that both Isaiah and John describe is the world where the lion lies down with the lamb; where swords are made into plowshares; where war is no more, and death is defeated. This is the true Christian hope based in the unchanging promise of God made at Mt. Sinai – you will be my people, and I will be your God.

It's easy to forget that promise if you watch the news, though. Just when you think you've heard it all, it seems that somewhere, someone will find ever more creative ways to exemplify evil. Our leaders will find new and improved ways to deceive us. The culture will find new and improved ways of seducing us to believe that redemption comes in the form of a large house and a 42-inch plasma screen television with 1000 channels of programming that we can program as we drive down the highway in our new and improved car.

As I was preparing for this morning, I read several articles and commentaries about these passages – and one of them stuck with me. A group of Lutheran scholars met to discuss how to preach from Revelation beginning with Easter Sunday and ending with Pentecost. They suggested the passage we read this morning as the text for the Sunday before Pentecost. Which is an interesting choice. Just before Pentecost, the disciples were still in shock from Jesus' death and resurrection – they still hadn't sorted out what it all meant. They huddled in fear in the Upper Room – not sure what they were waiting for.

I think those Lutheran scholars got this one right – this is a great passage for those of us who are huddled in our own upper rooms, not sure what to make of what's going on, afraid of what might be coming. These passages we read this morning tell us exactly what's coming – and that ultimately, we have nothing to fear. And our mourning will cease – there will, as Eric Clapton says, be no tears in heaven. God made a promise to Abraham, to the children of Israel at Mt. Sinai, through Jesus in his death and resurrection – and these passages remind us that God does not break promises. God's word is true – we can count on it.

But remember those children of Israel? After Sinai, everything wasn't warm and fuzzy after that. There were water shortages. People died. There were snakes. There was no food. The people grumbled. The people complained to Moses that this wasn't what they signed up for – they wanted to go back to Egypt where they might have been slaves, but at least they had food to eat. Every time they complained, God solved their problems – but not necessarily in the way they had asked. They needed food – they got manna. The manna wasn't quite enough – so they got quail once a week. They needed water – it came from rocks. They prayed to reach the promised land safely, and when they got there, they had to work a bit to get it. But the stories of their time in the wilderness tell us that despite God's work to save them, the people were hardly ever satisfied and went about trying to solve their own problems, making things new all on their own.

The ultimate question posed by Revelation is this: who is in control of the world? Where is power located? Which version of reality should we accept – the one offered to us by ad agencies, the government, television and movies – maybe even our religious leaders? Or the reality offered by God? Do we really want a new heaven and new earth designed by God?

Several years ago, Alice Seabold's book *The Lovely Bones* won lots of awards, and lots of acclaim. I think it was even an Oprah Book Club pick – and it was a good book. But part of the book's appeal for lots of readers was the description of heaven. If you haven't read the book I don't want to give away anything, but this young girl narrates the story from heaven. **Her** heaven – which is inhabited only by her. She gets visitors now and then, but it's explained to her that everyone gets their own heaven – their version of the perfect world. I won't go into the existential questions posed by the notion that if it's so perfect why she is still concerned about things happening on earth.... But that's the premise – we get to design our own heaven.

And I think we find that very attractive – designing our own heaven. Each of us has a different idea of what we think heaven will be like.

My nephew is concerned he might not like heaven – his mother told him that we would spend our days in heaven singing and worshipping God, and he informed her he gets bored in church – would there be activity books for kids?

But we think like that – whether we admit it or not, we suspect we might get bored day after day, into eternity. So, we daydream about what we might do in heaven – and with whom we might do it. Personally, I have a list of ten questions I want answered – starting with who was on that grassy knoll in Dallas in 1963 and just where IS Jimmy Hoffa?

But we don't have to daydream about what IS in heaven – John is very clear about what ISN'T in heaven – no tears, no death, no mourning, no crying, no pain – everything that we tend to focus on in this life – gone. Even the sea – which for John, imprisoned on an island, represented the separation from everything he loved – the sea is no more. All the former things are passed away – everything is new.

Isaiah goes one step further – he not only tells us what will Not be there (tears, disgrace, a shroud of death) but also tells us what WILL be there: a feast of rich food, well-aged wines – a party.

Both John and Isaiah were writing to people who were having a hard time holding on to the promise of God. John to people living under Roman rule, Isaiah to people who had been carried into exile in Babylon. And both give us this message – we know things are bad. The news – it's not good. Everything you hear, everything you fear is sending messages that while you trust in God, you should make other arrangements, cover all your bases, save yourself. But both John and Isaiah make this clear – only God can make things new, save us, usher in a time when there are no tears. Where we no longer must remember saints gone on before us – for we are all in one place. Where God will say – it is done, it's over, you no longer need to fear, to cry, to mourn, to hide. Time means nothing, for God is the beginning and the end.

I don't claim to understand all that – we don't have to. We claim our faith is mysterious – great is the mystery of faith we repeat each time we share communion. And we also claim that the risen Lord, who died for saints in every time and place, was God dwelling with us on earth for a time, but that when the kingdom comes, God will dwell with us on earth for all time.

Friends – this is what we pray for when we pray – thy kingdom come. Not the one we designed – the one God promised. The one where we will say – with all the saints – this is our God – we have waited and now we are saved.

This is the Lord for whom we have waited – let us be glad and rejoice in his salvation.

Jars of Clay
1 Thessalonians 5.1-11

You must give the apostle Paul a bit of credit – he can sound a bit like a snippy nanny, a bit preachy, a bit condescending at times. And to the Thessalonians, he was a bit of all those things. Paul loved these folks, but also thought they had a bit of a problem. They, it seemed, were convinced that Christ was returning Any. Day. Now. And because of that, there was nothing they needed to do other than wait around for that to happen. And not much else.

They were, for all intents and purposes, asleep at the wheel.

At this season of thanksgiving, as we move into Advent and then Christmas, it's easy to see where the Thessalonians were coming from. We're living in a world where we are congratulating ourselves for teaching school children to be so good at dealing with an active shooter situation that no one was killed in a recent shooting at an elementary school in California. We're living in a world where one of the corner discussions at Thursday's presbytery meeting was whether to lock the church doors during worship to protect ourselves. Where there is a discussion of whether it's appropriate to use "merry Christmas" at the mall (and if you don't get the irony of that discussion, see me later). Where the world seems to be going crazier all the time.

It's hard to be thankful. And pretty tempting to sit down on our ash heap and tend to our wounds while we wait for it all to be over. Pull the covers up over our head and hunker down. And be thankful that at least things here aren't as bad as they are somewhere else.

But friends, as followers of Christ that's not the example that was set for us. And Paul calls out the Thessalonians for their non-alertness.

As children of God, part of our call is a call to awake-ness – to pay attention, to see what needs doing. To be alert. To watch for...what, exactly? If you read the rest of this letter to the church, Paul spells out some specific things, and to sum it up, Pauls says: be like Christ. Be imitators of Christ. Comfort the afflicted, afflict the comfortable, feed the hungry, tend to the sick, challenge the status quo, eat and socialize with those on the margins – and generally be known by the way we love.

And this is not easy – especially not in a world that tends to value toughness, individualism, self-determination. As humans we often spend our time on guard one way or another. Guarding our feelings, our possessions, our lives.

But Paul reminds us that regardless of our efforts to protect ourselves and our stuff, the reality is we are fragile. We carry, Paul says, death in our bodies – these earthen vessels, jars of clay, is how one translation puts it. The Ash Wednesday liturgy tells us that we begin to die the moment we are born – that these human bodies carry death even as they live. They are extremely fragile, these jars of clay. But these fragile containers also carry the great gift of God: grace and love. And that God has gifted these fragile containers with so great a gift speaks of enormous trust and love – so much so that he entrusted his beloved Son to one of those jars of clay.

But even though the container is fragile, it is not unprotected, says Paul. We are also given the armor of God: the breastplate of faith and love, and the helmet of hope. Notice these are not weapons – this is protective gear that guards our hearts and minds. And this armor is made up of the only things Paul believes will outlast these jars of clay: faith, hope, and love. And we are protected because we have work to do. You, Paul tells the, are children of the day, children of the light. Others have reason to hide in the dark, fearing what is to come, but not you. You have work to do, which is why we have the protection.

As children of the light, children of the day, we are to be the light that shines in the darkness for others. But we are often content to let others do it. I know I have been complicit more than once in letting the darkness linger – until someone else drags it out. Then I get on board and joyfully embrace the light.

Friends, we should not rely on news organizations to root out the blight of sexual harassment and predatory behavior. We should not depend on social services to discover abused and neglected children. We can't expect those in power to protect the innocent. These are things we, as imitators of Christ, should be doing. If we are walking in the light, we should also be walking in places that need that light.

This is what the Thessalonians were NOT doing – they were content to take their position as children of God and protect it. But Paul was warning them: if you aren't out there sharing the light with those that sit in darkness, then you WILL be surprised when the Day of the Lord comes. And it might not be so pleasant. When you believe you have secured peace and security – Paul says: "then sudden destruction will come upon them."

Okay, this is sounding like there's not much here to inspire thankfulness, and I can hear you thinking: Pastor, get to the thankful thing. Please. It's getting late.

There **is** much to be thankful for, as children of the light. We have the breastplate of faith and love, and the helmet of hope, which in a world that wants to capture our hearts and minds, are no small things. But here's the real gift, Paul says: children of the light, children of God, we don't need to worry about what comes next, what comes after. We are destined, not for wrath, but for salvation.

We have, in short, nothing to fear.

What a gift that is in a world designed to make us fearful.

At presbytery Thursday, Jan Edmiston, who is co moderator of the General Assembly, had a question and answer session. One of the questions was about security during church services in the wake of the Texas church shooting. I thought her answer was one Paul would have liked: she said we can't protect ourselves from every threat in the world, and that the church was meant to be open and welcoming to others, all others. And if someone wanted to take her life, her faith was in a God more powerful and loving than any security system.

That, friends, seems like an answer that knows we hold a treasure in a fragile, earthen vessel. But the treasure is not the vessel – it is the grace with which we are infused, life and death of Christ that gives us the protection of faith, hope and love. The things that let us walk confidently out in the open, in the light, rather than hiding in the dark, waiting for rescue.

Thanks be to God.

Metamorphosis

Luke 9.28-36; 2 Corinthians 3.12-4.2

Luke's gospel, frankly, is my favorite of the four. It has the best parables, lots of chatty details that aren't in the other three gospels, and Luke divides Jesus' public ministry into two sections – before he sets his face toward Jerusalem, and after.

In the verses directly before this morning's passage – verses 21 through 27 – Jesus is giving his disciples the rest of the story. They've been following Jesus around the country, preaching, teaching, healing, and generally getting good reviews. But there is more.

Which is this: Jesus is headed directly into rejection, suffering and certain death, and there is a real chance that the rest of them are, too. Heavy stuff. And so, we come to today's passage – Jesus and three handpicked disciples headed up the mountain to pray. A short side trip to restore and rejuvenate the soul.

This short trip turned out to be more than the disciples expected, I think. They headed up the mountain for a bit of rest and relaxation and now Jesus is now talking with the great prophets of Israel about his own death. But, once again, we can count on Peter to bring the proper amount of enthusiasm to the event. If Luke is my favorite gospel, Peter is my favorite disciple, because he just is so.... Human.

Immediately, Peter wants to build three buildings – one each for Jesus, Moses and Elijah. These would be a sort of chapel dedicated to each of them. For Peter, this trip has been an experience that he wants to hold on to. No doubt he felt this was the messiah he signed on with – no more talk of death and suffering. At this point, I'd like to imagine a hand reaching out to give Peter a "you are missing the point – again" head slap. Sort of a divine NCIS moment. But alas, Luke does not tell us of a head slap.

But during Peter's excitement, a cloud rolled in and the voice from heaven told them – and Jesus – "This is my son, my chosen.... Listen to him."

How tempting it must have been for Jesus to agree with Peter, help build those worship booths and stay there where there were no crowds to feed, sick to heal or demons to cast out. No imminent suffering and death. But there was work to do. And things on the journey would begin to take a different turn from this point. The journey that takes Jesus to Jerusalem takes us into Lent.

The American Heritage Dictionary says that transfiguration means a **marked change in form or appearance; a metamorphosis**. Word net defines it as a striking change in appearance or character or circumstances; as in "the metamorphosis of the old into something new and exciting." (which seems especially on point here) Transfiguration is the event that begins the process of metamorphosis.[2]

That striking change – transfiguration – may look different to each of us, depending on the circumstances subject to change. For some, it's the death of a spouse or parent; the loss of a job; a lump in a breast....

Or maybe your best friend telling you that he must go to Jerusalem where they will kill him, and maybe kill you, too; or maybe it's knowing that if you go to Jerusalem they will kill you, and your friends don't understand.

Whatever it is, that moment of transfiguration is a pivot point in life – things will never again look quite the same. And we can't always see that there is a metamorphosis going on – the pain of loss or the fear of sacrifice can keep us from remembering that there is a

---

[2]https://www.ahdictionary.com/word/search.html?q=transfiguration)

gracious God with a plan. But just as on this mountain, God provides a glimpse of glory so that even though things are changed, we can go on.

Jesus went to that mountaintop knowing that his closest friends did not truly understand. This mountaintop experience was Jesus' refueling – the granting of peace – so that he could return to the work laid out for him. And while Peter and the other disciples might not have understood the significance of this transfiguration – the Scripture says they kept silent about those events – never the less the metamorphosis had begun. These three disciples would carry on the ministry of Jesus at the point of death and the journey to Jerusalem would become an exodus into freedom for all of humankind. But none of that was clear that night on the mountain. It was a transfiguration, but the metamorphosis had only begun.

Peter wanted to build some worship booths and hold on to that mountain experience, but the revelation of Jesus' humanity and divinity was not to be hoarded. Once we know who Jesus truly is, we can't stay in the glow of glory – we must move forward. An exodus toward freedom isn't an exodus if we stay put.

Paul put it this way in 2 Corinthians: *Since then, we have such a hope, we act with great boldness.*

When you see the glory, you can't be the same. While it was Jesus who was transfigured on that mountaintop, it was the disciples who began the process of metamorphosis. These bumbling followers who needed a cosmic head slap would eventually die martyr's deaths of their own.

Paul refers to the story of Moses on Mt. Sinai, receiving the law from God. When Moses came down from the mountain, his face was shining with the reflected glory of God – and the people were afraid to come near him. So, Moses put a veil over his face, which he would take off when he was in God's presence.

That is one of those things that makes me go Hmmmm. How many people get close to the glory of God, and then hide it? How many people do we know who have been given a glimpse of the divine power and sovereignty of God, but it changes nothing. Moses allowed the fear of the people to mask the truth of God's power. And that was Peter's first thought: let's leave this here – where we can come revisit it when we want, but don't have to carry that truth with us along the road. It could get heavy, burdensome to know these things. But the instructions to the disciples are also instructions to us: This is my son, listen to him.

The truth of who Jesus is and was is not a possession to be guarded. It was – and is – a gift to be shared.

This week, we begin the journey into Lent – a time when we look inside ourselves, meditate, pray – to consider the gift of Jesus and his willingness to be the sacrificial lamb on our behalf. Of the vulnerable God who died so that death might be defeated.

The gift of the Good News of God – it is this good news that allows us to know that whatever the striking change in circumstances, the sovereignty of God is unchanging. As we move into the season of Lent, we move from the mountaintop back into the trenches, bringing with us the knowledge of who Jesus truly was and is.

And then and now, the instructions are the same: This is my son, my chosen. Listen to him……

As we prepare to come to the table Christ has set for us, let us come knowing that the moment of transfiguration has come – and the metamorphosis has begun. What we will be, what we will learn during this season, we can't know. But we can know this: We have been given a gift to share, and we can't share it if we stay where we are.

The Faith to Step Up
Luke 7.1-10

Faith is a word that gets bandied about often. In the last couple of decades, you will find more people talking about faith during election cycles than at most other times. It seems the way to get elected any more is to have more faith than the next person. And the right kind of faith – we tend to have a checklist of what you "have" to believe to be "faithful."

And there are folks – most of them have tv shows – who are talking about faith as something that, if you just have enough, can be traded in for the desires of your heart. Sort of like an ATM. But it's on you to "have enough." If you don't have enough faith, then the miracles don't come, things don't change, you don't live your best life…

But faith – the kind of faith I want to talk about today – is both simpler and more complicated than that. It's not a checklist. It's not a series of "if…then" statements. It's not a gauge by which we measure our closeness to God. It's something else.

This incident that Luke gives us this morning – it stands out for a couple of reasons. Luke tends to give us more details, more stories than the other gospel writers. Jesus has just finished the sermon on the mount, and now Luke sort of gives us a travelogue of where Jesus went, and what happened. And as he entered Capernaum, he is met by a welcoming party of local religious leaders. Generally, Jesus wasn't met by religious leaders who were happy he was there. Jesus tended to stir things up, but this group had a request. They needed Jesus to help a friend of theirs – a Roman centurion, of all things. This Roman officer had a slave that was very sick, and had heard of Jesus, and knew that Jesus could heal this slave.

This centurion, military officer charged with keeping the peace in the area, is an interesting character. He apparently had built the local synagogue – which could have been part of keeping the peace, but it's likely he was what religious leaders of the time called "God fearers" – people who were attracted to the monotheistic Jewish religion but weren't quite ready to fully convert. There were apparently lots of these folks.

We often think that because the Romans worshipped many gods that they weren't as religious as the Jews – but this isn't the case. In fact, many Romans were very religious, and the prospect of one God more powerful than any other would have had some appeal. So, this centurion knew about Jesus and his powers of healing.

Because he had been instrumental in building the local church, this centurion could have leveraged his power to get to Jesus. He could have used the power of his generosity – or even his power as a centurion – to meet Jesus and escort him directly to his house. He had rank to pull – but he did not. Instead, he let the community speak with and for him.

The power of community can be impressive. Early on Sunday mornings NPR airs *On Being* with Krista Tippit – and if you're not familiar with the show, I recommend it. This morning, the guest was writer Rebecca Solnit. The show promo describes her writing this way: She searches for the hidden, transformative histories inside events we chronicle merely as disasters, in places like post-Hurricane Katrina New Orleans. She writes that, so often, "when all the ordinary divides and patterns are shattered, people step up to become their brothers' keepers. And that purposefulness and connectedness bring joy even amidst death, chaos, fear, and loss."[3]

Solnit says that hope is often seen as weakness, but the vulnerability required to be part of a redemptive community requires a kind of strength that isn't often rewarded in our culture of rugged individualism.

---

[3] From the "On Being" website promo for the May 29, 2016 episode. https://onbeing.org/

This centurion, who commanded soldiers and literally held the power of life and death over those around him, knew that the power of the community – the connectedness of our humanity – was key. He may not have understood completely why, but he knew that his faith in the context of a community of faith was stronger than his alone and made it easier to step out in and on that faith.

Faith is not a solitary endeavor – and it is never for our own benefit or gain. The centurion stepped out in faith with the community on behalf of someone who could not. Spoke on behalf of one that had no voice – a slave. Had hope on behalf of one that may not have had hope of their own. This centurion, as Rebecca Solnit puts it, stepped up to be his brother's keeper.

This passage begins with the words: When Jesus had finished his sayings in the hearing of all the people. Another translation puts it this way: when Jesus had filled the people's ears with his sayings… Filled their ears.

The "sayings" referred to here is the sermon on the mount – the Lukan version. And that ended with the comparison of the wise and the foolish men who built houses – one on the sand, the other on solid rock. That comparison was preceded by this: 'Why do you call me "Lord, Lord", and do not do what I tell you? I will show you what someone is like who comes to me, hears my words, and acts on them.'

There is a clear line that connects hearing and acting – and this story of the centurion shows that line. Those of us who preach and believe in justification by faith alone – and I'm one of those – often get a bit shy about talking about works of faith. It makes us nervous. But question 86 of the Heidelberg Catechism asks this: Since we have been delivered from our misery by grace alone through Christ, without any merit of our own, why must we yet do good?

And the answer is this: Because Christ, having redeemed us by his blood also renews us by his Holy Spirit to be his image, so that with our whole life we may show ourselves thankful to God.

But I think Rebecca Solnit may have hit on another reason – the works of a community of faith connect us on a deeper level, and that connectedness, that faith lived out in the world – it's the source of a genuine hope, genuine gratitude. It makes it easier to live out the words of Jesus from his sermon: But I say to you that listen, love your enemies, do good to those who hate you, bless those who curse you, pray for those who abuse you. To judge not. To forgive. To give – not for what we get out of it, but for what it puts into the world: hope.

Jesus held up this centurion as an example of faith – great faith. And it's no accident, I think, that this story is placed just after the sermon on the mount that challenges us to act in faith – to be doers of the word, and not hearers only.

It is in the doing that purposefulness – regardless of circumstances – can lead to joy. Lead to hope.

Living Stones
Acts 7.55-60; 1 Peter 2.1-10

One of the gifts of the Presbyterians to the world of established church is our form of polity – which, frankly, is both blessing and curse. But one thing the new form of government approved in 2011 does is make clear, in no uncertain terms, that the head of the church is Christ.

We tend to think of "my church," and when we say that, we usually mean a collection of people, a specific building, maybe even a set of programs. But I wonder if that thinking is deep enough.

This morning, this short passage from Acts describes the death of Stephen – and illustrates how in a fairly short time, followers of Jesus have gone from a bunch of frightened people who ran away and hid out in locked rooms, to a group that would die for what they believe.

A voluntary association of people or a building, or even a great program probably wouldn't create that kind of dedication. How did an interesting collection of frightened and confused people become the church that would affect the whole world?

Peter offers a clue – the church is made up of God's own people, called and claimed. Transformed into living stones that build something unshakable. The real bricks and mortar of the church is not what shelters us – it is us. Built into a community of believers.

It is the community that makes us God's people, the community that makes us able to proclaim the mighty acts of God, the community that provides the framework for God to form us and transform us – to bring us out of exile and bondage and into the promised freedom.

But not for our own sakes solely. This Community is created by God – so that we might be God's people.

Peter, who would have been very familiar with the Hebrew scriptures, uses the idea of God's chosen people in telling believers who they are and what they are to be. Peter, who listened to Jesus tell over and over again how he came to fulfill the law, would know the words God used when giving the law to Moses at Mt. Sinai – from Exodus 19: You shall be my own possession from among all peoples; for all the earth is mine; and you shall be to me a kingdom of priests, and a holy nation.'

Last week we talked about what makes a church different from a country club – this week, what makes us able to be different from a country club. Peter – who is writing to believers who are facing persecution that could end very much like Stephen ended, wants to make clear that the faith we have does not come from within us. It comes from a powerful God who calls, and when God calls, God transforms and enables.

Living stones, Peter called the people.

So, the saga of my flower bed in the back yard continues – and I've planted some lovely things in it but had not counted on the fact that once you take out of the sandy dirt the things you don't want planted in there, it leaves the soil open to being washed directly into the driveway. So, after some thinking and planning and wishin' and hopin', I think I have a plan. And it involves some edging stones along the lower side of the bed, which I hope will keep the rest of the flower bed from ending up across the street with the next big rain.

Because stones can serve a variety of uses. As a wall, they can hold back things. Protect things. Cut things off from the rest of the world. Bricks and mortar as we normally use them aren't all that portable – there's some serious heft to them. That's why we use them.

But bricks alone, stones alone – they aren't always stable. They need something to hold them together. When I put those edging stones along my flower bed, I'm going to have to stabilize them somehow. And a pile of bricks with no mortar – is just a pile of bricks.

Bricks, stones need something to hold them together.

And Peter is clear: the mortar that holds the living stones together is Christ. And here's the miracle of the transformation that happens when Christ is the mortar of a ragtag group of believers, whether it's in first century Palestine, or 21st century Palestine IL: we become something more than the sum of our parts.

The downside of bricks and mortar establishments – like this building – is it is stationary. It can't move. But the lovely things about being living stones in the church that Christ built is this:

The mortar that binds us – Christ – allows us to be a community that lives and moves and has our being in Christ. Allows us to move out of the buildings we construct and go out into the world and into our community.

The constricting thing about real stones and mortar is that it's a finite size – with all the storage problems, and badly used space, and upkeep costs that go along with buildings. But as living stones, bound together into a community of believers, a spiritual house, a people for God's possession – we are not finite. Not bound by the constrictions of time, space – or any other boundary of the mortal world. We can go out into the world as a community, living stones who carry the light, who, because we have received mercy, can bring mercy to a merciless world.

For therefore we are called, bound together into a community: to remind ourselves and the world that God is a God of light, love and mercy. And we are where God has chosen to place that light, love and mercy. Not to hoard it – but to share it. To shower the world with it.

This week, one of the economic stories is the trouble retail stores are having in an age of Amazon and free shipping, and internet shopping. Retail stores rely on people's willingness to come to them and buy what they have on display. Internet shopping, however, means you can stay home, and search the whole interwebs, and if one place doesn't have what you want, Google will help you find another. And then it will come to you, rather than the other way around.

This is a good lesson for us as church. For most of our history, at least in this country, we have been able to depend on people coming to us, looking to get what we have. But that isn't the case any longer – and it wasn't the case when Peter was writing. As followers of Christ, called, chosen, and gifted with light and mercy, we are to go out into the world.

This is our call as church, our identity as church – that we go, not as a static, bricks and mortar building that houses and protects the truth. But as a living community who showers the world with truth and light, as we have been showered with it.

May we go – filled with light and mercy – as the people of God. The Community of love.

The Message

Luke 2.41-52

Praise.

Praise in the psalm of the day. Praise in the gospel reading for the day. Praise in the prophet reading for the day. Praise even in the epistle for the day. Praise – the time of waiting is over, Christ has come.

But we're probably tired from all those preparations – because this is the reality of our lives. Advent is a time of preparation, but not for the divine incarnation so much. Yes, there's that, but generally that happens as part of our other preparations: meals, houses, decorations, presents, family gatherings… And those preparations tend to wear us out.

And then there's just the general wearing out that life does to us. We live in a world and in a time that is wearing. Violence – and then the protests against the violence lead to more violence. A world where imagining anything different is hard, because it just seems as if nothing really changes for the better, that we are simply headed in a direction that can't be changed. That nothing really ever changes. We celebrated the birth of a baby that was supposed to change everything, and we emerge from Christmas morning tired, facing news stories that continue to tell us there is much to fear, that there is much to despair, and our only hope is to hunker down and hope it all passes.

But this morning, we need to remember that the baby in the manger is part of a never-ending story. The Christ that has come, will come. We move from the waiting of Advent and toward the waiting of Pentecost. And in this in between time, we have this story of Simeon and Anna who have been waiting to see the promise of God come to fulfillment.

These two demonstrate the tension in which we live in these days: the fulfillment of the past, the immediacy of the present and the expectation of the future. Living in the tension of these three is how we are able to raise our voices in praise in a world that seems to be careening out of control – with so much to fear, so much to lament, so much designed to drain our hope and move us toward despair.

Simeon and Anna recognize this tension. The presence of Mary, Joseph and Jesus at the temple is part of this tension.

This visit to the Temple was a regular part of Jewish life. We know very little about Jesus' childhood, and the stories we have demonstrate that Jesus was born into a Jewish home that took the Jewish traditions and rituals seriously. Forty days after the birth of a child, the family presents the child at the temple, offers a sacrifice – and completes the purification rituals associated with childbirth. This is ordinary and expected. But Luke wants us to see beyond the traditions of the past, which are important, and beyond the reality of the present, which are necessary, and into the possibility of the future, and the ways these are all tied together.

Simeon's hymn – for it is a song – is used in graveside interment services. Lord, dismiss your servant in peace. It's also part of the daily prayer service used at the close of day. While Simeon is relieved that he has seen the promise of the Messiah, it's clear that he understands that while his work/watching is done, the story is not over. Simeon knows his part in the story – standing watch, bearing witness and proclaiming the truth. And knows that the story continues and can stand and offer praise for what has gone before, what is, and what is to come.

The prophet Anna has also been waiting to see the fulfillment of God's promise that came through earlier prophets, including Isaiah – that God will deliver Israel from despair and sow joy and praise where there is none. She had been praying and waiting – and when she saw the child, she realized that the story was not finished. She continued to bear witness, to share the good news that what had been promised had been fulfilled, but there is much to anticipate.

Isaiah uses the metaphor of gardening – and he's not the only prophet that uses this metaphor – for the on-going story of God's work in and for the world. To be a satisfied gardener, you must be able to live in the tension between what was, what is and what will be. To garden, you must understand the nature of hope – to live in the infinite possibilities that transcend past and present.

I'm a bad gardener – but I apparently raised a good one. He would cringe to hear me describe it this way, but my son is living his life in a theologically hopeful way. Despite his tales of woe about being subjected to planting and weeding tomatoes and flowers when he was younger, these days he harvests and dries his own seeds, painstakingly oversees those seeds becoming sprouts during the waning days of winter, lovingly tends to his herb and vegetable garden, and cans or uses nearly everything that he grows. The story of a garden is an ongoing story that relies on past, present and future. The work of a gardener is inherently hopeful – regardless of what phase of gardening you happen to be in now.

Gardeners understand that for new possibilities to emerge, old realities must die. Yet we can't reject out of hand what has gone before – the learnings of past seasons carry into the current plantings. The richness of the soil, cultivated in the past and over time, is necessary to the success of what is currently growing. And we know that the tomatoes we harvest today are only here for a season. And even in the preserving of today's harvest for tomorrow, there is still a need to plant again. And harvest again. And cultivate again. The possibilities go on and on, and each year, each season, brings a new set of possibilities. Some harvests are bumper crops, some are devoured by locusts. But we never will know until we plant. We stand this morning at the beginning of the journey between Advent and Pentecost – from one waiting to another – knowing that the story does not end. Doesn't end with the birth of a baby, the death of a rabbi, the resurrection of a savior – in fact, each of these simply begins the story again, opening ever more possibilities.

It is easy, however to become convinced that the important thing here is the gardener – that we are the primary agent at work. Anna and Simeon knew that they had important work, important witness. But they were aware that the story both preceded and outlasted their mortal lives. The promise of God, the story of God's work in the world, goes on. That hope is ever present, for God's promises, while given to each of us individually, are for the whole world in every time and place.

This is the good news – that the story, regardless of how hopeless it seems, is not over. And it's not all up to us. There are infinite possibilities, and they are not limited by what we see, what we imagine. Anna and Simeon saw a baby and knew that this child would lead to the redemption of the world – even though the personal story for this child and his mother would not have a happy ending. The story is bigger – and the hope is bigger.

So, let us carry out into the world that the baby has come, that hope endures. For this is the good news – in a world where there is much to fear, we can carry the message: Fear not.

Faith: It's More than Wishin' and Hopin'
Genesis 17.1-7, 15-16; Romans 4.13-25

Covenant seems to be a theme for this Lenten season. Last week, it was the covenant God made after the flood – which seems especially pertinent this week. This week, the covenant with Abraham. While the covenant with Noah was to never again destroy the earth because of the evil doings of humans, the covenant with Abraham has a slightly different tone – this time, God makes a covenant of reconciliation with humans. And through this one man, Abraham, to reconcile all nations, all people back to God.

I don't know about you, but I'm glad that worked out so well, aren't you? Because humanity is so much more reconciled – to God and to one another, right?

Now that that's done, we can put all this self-examination of Lent over to the side and move on to the celebration of resurrection. Except that we can't.

Abraham's journey wasn't over – there was still a journey to be taken, mistakes to be made, sacrifices to be offered – including the precious son of the promise, Isaac – and Abraham himself would never see the multitude of nations reconciled to God and to one another. In fact, I'm not sure I will ever see it.

But one of the things that came out of our Wednesday night study of Psalms was this observation from scholar J. Clinton McCann about the perspective of the psalms: they declare God's universal reign amid circumstances that seem to deny it and belie it.[4] And as Paul tells the church in Rome, Abraham's faith was not a faith that was based on what he had seen God do – because at this point, he and Sara were still childless, Abraham still had some major boneheaded mistakes to make, and there was no reason to believe

---

[4] NIB commentary, Vol. IV; p 668 (Abingdon Press, 1990)

that the promise of God was to be believed. Yet Abraham did believe, and when God told him to start moving toward a place he did not know and could not describe, Abraham did.

A faith built on nothing less than a promise.

A hope built on nothing more than faith.

As I've been reading and studying for the Wednesday night Lent study on psalms, I keep running across references and readings about the prosperity gospel. If you're not familiar with it – and I bet you are, even if you don't call it that. Prosperity gospel is based on the belief that God wants us to prosper, and if we just have enough faith, pray hard enough, believe, God will give us not only what we need, but we will also prosper – and prosper by all the definitions you can give that word: money, success, popularity. And the best preachers of this gospel prosper very well: big houses, big salaries, big entourages, big buildings. Everything is big.

But this is a false gospel – God DOES want us to prosper, but God does not define prosperity the same way we might. And a gospel based on how hard we pray, how deep our faith might be, or how well we can live according to the rules and regulations is a gospel that cheapens the reality of the gospel of Christ – the Christ that lived, died and rose again.

But that's not the point this morning – I bring it up only to make this point: there is a brand of faith that teaches that you can measure faith by the results you see and experience. If your faith is deep enough, then the results of that faith can be measured by the quality of your own life.

But I don't think that's what God promised to Abraham, and that's not what Paul was telling the Romans. God's covenant with Abraham was for the future – Abraham would never see the multitude of ancestors promised, would not be the patriarch of a nation while he was around to be in charge. And it was not dependent on Abraham's ability to do the right thing.

Which is a good thing, because like most of the people chosen by God as actors in God's work in the world, Abraham had feet of clay – and kept trying to take control of the process of the promise. But despite his mistakes, Abraham kept putting one foot in front of the other, headed toward a place he did not know, but that God promised to lead him. And this willingness to follow, Paul tells the Romans, was reckoned to him as righteousness.

Righteousness – the rightness of ourselves. Which, Paul tells us elsewhere, no one can get on their own. It doesn't matter how hard we pray, how much faith we have, how deep our belief if we aren't willing to put one foot in front of the other and move out into the places God leads. It isn't about our willingness to follow the rules, or keep traditions, or do things decently and in order, as Presbyterians are fond of saying.

The church to which Paul was writing was a combination of Jewish and Gentile believers. The Jewish believers saw themselves as the true believers – custodians of the faith, if you will. And that to be a good Christian, you had to follow Mosaic law. The gentiles, on the other hand, came to God only through Jesus, and rejected the notion that Mosaic law had anything of value.

Paul took them both to task, but ultimately comes down here: the law can point out our need for faith, but the law is no substitute for faith. For just like with Abraham, it is our faith that reckons for us righteousness, not our ability to follow laws or rules, or even commandments. And Paul points out that Abraham's faith grew, not through actions or rule-keeping, but from giving glory to God and remaining convinced that God was able to do what God had promised.

Now sometimes, Abraham decided that God might need a bit of help here and there, but Abraham never doubted that God's promise was one that would be kept. But that human impatience often got in his way.

Which, I think, is one reason these passages are here, in the second week of Lent. We begin Lent with the deep awareness of Ash Wednesday, and during the first week continue that reflection. But by this second Sunday, our human impatience has started to pop up. I don't know about you, but I'm ready to move on to the triumphant entry on Palm Sunday and get to the celebration of Easter. I'm weary of self-reflection.

But I think Paul is warning us this morning: you must finish this journey.

The gospel passage in this week's lectionary is from Mark, just after Peter has made his declaration of who he believes Jesus to be. And when Jesus tells his followers, his friends, that he must suffer and die, Peter gets upset. So just a few verses after Jesus promises to build his church on Peter's faith, Jesus tells him: get behind me, Satan!

Peter and the others didn't get a shortcut on the journey. Abraham didn't get a shortcut. Paul didn't get a shortcut. We must walk the pathway before us – even if we aren't entirely sure we are going to like the neighborhood it goes through.

Taken together, these passages affirm the need to journey all forty days of Lent. The faith it takes to spend this time considering our own frailty, our own propensity for mischief, our own lack of ability to save ourselves – this is the kind of faith that reckons to us righteousness. This is the kind of faith that understands that the only way to have a rightly oriented life is to acknowledge our dependence on God – and that God is infinitely powerful, yet infinitely loving. And that this powerful, loving being is willing to direct all that power and love toward us, making something of nothing, just as God did at the beginning.

In this second stop in the journey of Lent, I challenge you this week to consider the faith of Abraham – which was a faith that began and ended in his belief that God was able and willing to keep a promise. And that faith grew – despite never seeing the results in his own lifetime.

Can we have that kind of faith? The kind of faith that lets us put one foot in front of the other without knowing the destination? The kind that isn't measured by the amount of "prosperity" we enjoy? The kind that can be reckoned as righteousness?

I believe we can…

Why Can't We All Just Get Along?
Acts 4.32-33; Psalm 133

How wonderful it is when we live together as family – right? And as church, we love to call ourselves family – feel like family, treat one another like family…

I don't know about your family, but I'd rather not have another group treat me like family. I get enough of that on holidays and at the Olive Garden. Because, being a family can be tough. You know all their faults, all their buttons that are so much fun to push. You live in close quarters with people you might not like but are forced to love. And it can be emotionally messy – there is an entire class of therapy called Marriage and Family Therapy, and there's a reason for that. We will say and do things to family we'd never say or do to anyone else.

So yeah, church is like family. Who wouldn't want to be part of that?

Psalm 133, which celebrates the delights of unity, is a psalm of ascents, which means it was sung as people went up to the temple. And the poetic images of the psalm hides for us the perplexing paradoxes in this hymn of praise to living together.

First – living in unity is like oil poured out upon the head. Now, in ancient times, this was a good thing. In the desert, regular showers weren't commonly available, so there were other ways of being able to live in close quarters with one another, and one of those ways was scented oils. But in this psalm, it could be too much of a good thing. The oil isn't just poured on the head, it's poured out in a large amount, going down the face, down the neck – all over. No doubt creating quite a mess. I think of this as weaponized hospitality.

And the dew of Hermon falling on the mountains of Zion – well that's two different countries. And while it could happen, it seems unlikely. And maybe even unwelcome since it's also probably two different climates. Kind of like us having northern Canada's weather now.

So, when you strip down those examples, living together like kindred, like family, is either like having too much of a good thing to the point that it creates an aggravation, or so unlikely as to never happen.

That tracks with my experience – how about you?

The psalmist KNOWS that living in unity is difficult – but also is clear about this: this is what the Lord wants for us. This is the place where the Lord's blessing lies. Which also tracks with my experience – family is exasperating – but at the end of the day, can also be the source of great blessing.

So yeah, church is like family – and I DO want to be part of that.

The earliest believers were Jews who would have known this psalm, and were in peril, not just from the Romans, but had also been ostracized by their fellow Jews. In some cases, the company of believers were likely all some believers had – and their family of faith had become their new family. And so, they lived together as family – sharing all their stuff, sharing space, sharing…. everything.

And the passage from Acts stops there this morning, the place where everything was good. Where they loved and laughed and shared and got along. It was indeed good and pleasant.

But like most situations where people try and live together in unity: it was both messy and unlikely. It didn't take very long for that kind of situation to fall apart. Don't get me wrong: I think they were trying to live out the teachings of Jesus in a real way. I think Jesus would love it if we loved one another enough to share everything we had with everyone else and were able to share space without having our personal preferences and personalities intrude. I suspect this is the way Jesus and his followers lived as they travelled around. And I suspect these early days of the church were the apostles trying to replicate the life they had with Jesus.

But this is the challenge of living in the light of the risen Lord – without the physical Jesus in our midst to make sure we don't go off the rails... well, we go off the rails. And before you know it, we are using our hospitality as a weapon (I'm talking about you Olive Garden) and living together in any kind of unity becomes as unlikely as snow the second week of April. It's possible – but who really enjoys that sort of thing?

The psalmist knew – and the first believers learned – that living together in unity is hard. It's messy. It's unlikely and goes against our nature. We are wired to look out for ourselves first and foremost – our most primal instincts are fight or flight, neither of which is particularly conducive to unity. Sharing our stuff – well, that's just hard. And the first believers learned that even when you WANT to share all things in common, we usually want to hold back a little something, just in case.

After the fourth chapter of Acts, you don't hear too much about the believers living in and having all things in common. And by the time Paul is starting churches in Asia Minor, there have been several kerfuffles about how to "be church" that resulted in uneasy compromises. And truthfully, if churches hadn't been full of people who were living together more like real families and less like the utopia described in Acts 4, we wouldn't have most of Paul's letters. There's not a lot of reason to keep a letter that says: ya'll are doing great. Keep it up.

But – circling back to the psalmist – living in unity and as kindred is where the blessing of God can be found. One of the great paradoxes of faith is that we are individually redeemed – but can only live as redeemed people in community with other redeemed people. The gospel lesson for today is the story of Thomas – who doubted the story that Jesus had risen from the dead. Jesus appeared, Thomas believed – but Jesus appeared to a group, the gathered community that believed. And in that context Thomas' doubt becomes the less important fact. What's important is that Thomas was still in that room with the people who believed – until he could believe on his own.

Nadia Bolz Weber said once that one of her parishioners came to her and said he had trouble saying the creed each week because he wasn't sure he believed all of it. Her response was this: well of course not. Nobody believes all the creed all the time. Some weeks parts of it are harder than others. But the reason we say it together is this: whichever part is giving you trouble this week, someone believes it. And each week, all the creed it believed by someone in the congregation. So together, all the creed is what we believe, together.

Because the truth is, it IS hard to live together in unity, hard to believe these hard to believe things, hard to live as followers of Jesus when Jesus isn't leading us down the actual road. But every week, at least some of us know that we are on the right track, following the right messiah.

And then – it is both pleasant and perplexing, veering off at times into vexing. But that's the messiness of unity – and where the blessings of God reside.

If There Be Any Encouragement….
Philippians 2.1-13

I would have liked to start today's message with the words: It's been an interesting couple of weeks in the news. But frankly, it's been a couple of weeks of more of the same.

More polarization. More division. More sniping. More lamenting over the state of things. More name calling. More threats. More irony to go along with all that.

And part and parcel with that is the jockeying for position – whether it's to be on the right side of an argument, the winning side of a game, aligned with the right people, set up for the proper optics. We are in a time and place that seems unprecedented in our distrust of one another, of our leaders, of the future. Hope has become a punchline in a Saturday Night Live skit – not something one should invest in. Better we invest in security and stability. Or maybe it's better that we hitch our wagon to the upsetters, the outsiders, the ones that want to shake things up.

To stand and declare that the only things that last are faith hope and love in a world that traffics only in fear, distrust and gamesmanship is the height of arrogance. Isn't it?

I know that for some reason it seems hard this week to read the words of Paul, who urges us to be in full accord and have one mind. I don't want to have one mind. I want to hunker down and watch Netflix under the covers. Or to find some like-minded people and spend all my time with them. Insulate myself from the potential divisions and difficulties – and hope that faith and love can be rekindled.

Unfortunately, these words of Paul's have followed me around all week. I was planning to speak this morning on the Old Testament reading: the water from a rock. That seems hopeful – God taking care of God's people in the wilderness. On Wednesday, that seemed like a good idea. But as the week went on, there seemed to be less to say. And then I re-read the words of Paul:

IF there be any encouragement in Christ.

I've often said, and stand by the statement, that the Bible is not a collection of If/Then propositions. If we do this, then God will do that. But in this case, Paul is making a rhetorical argument: if Christ is able to encourage us – both in the comforting and in the urging along meaning of that word, THEN there is something we should do: be of the same mind.

Yeah. Like that's gonna happen.

But Paul doesn't stop there. Have the same love, be of one accord – of one mind. And Paul gets down to it: the same mind that is in Christ. Which means we have to think about what Christ's mind set was and is. Or we don't, because Paul then launches into this old hymn about Christ and Christ's mind set:

He emptied himself and was born a human being. Humbled himself and was exalted.

Which is pretty much what Jesus himself said: If you try to save your life you will lose it, but if you lose your life you will save it. Take up your cross and follow me.

I have heard many interpretations of those words – commands if you like – and many lists of ways that should happen. But I think Paul has gotten to the heart of it as he writes to this church that he loved: Be of one mind; the mind of Christ.

See what Christ would see. Think what Christ would think. Do what Christ would do. Love the way Christ would love. Which seems hard. There is an awful lot of people and situations that I would prefer NOT to see as Christ might see them. I prefer my righteous indignation about it all, to be honest. My right-ness.

I often joke that my spiritual gift is the gift of discernment: I know how things ought to be. And when things aren't how I think they ought to be – or even more specifically, how I interpret scripture to think they ought to be, I can burn with the righteous anger that is purer than the white-hot heat of a thousand suns. Which is pretty darn righteous.

But Paul, who could also burn with a white hot righteous indignation that could scorch the earth, says: Nope. Look not to your own interests, but to the interests of others.

Which is hard. And I don't like to do hard things. In fact, as humans, wired the way we are for self-preservation, it's hard to put the interests of other ahead of ourselves. Everything about our physical, emotional, and psychic systems is geared to fight or flight – which means that having the same mind as Christ, to be in one accord, to have one love: this is not necessarily in our nature.

And Paul knew this, about the Philippians, about himself – and about us. And so, he reminds the Philippines, and me, and the rest of us: you are not in this alone. For God is working in you, enabling you to want to do this hard thing, and be able to do this hard thing.

Carrie Newcomber has a song, *Hard Thing*, and the chorus is this: You can do this hard thing, I know. And she credits writer Barbara Kingsolver for the inspiration, as that's something she told her children: you can do hard things.

Paul is telling the Philippians: you can do hard things. Because you aren't doing them alone.

Remember that Paul is writing to a church that is facing real and difficult persecution. The kind that isn't inconvenient, but deadly. Keep the faith, keep doing what you should be doing, Paul says.

Because when you keep the one love, the one accord, the one mind, then God is at work in you, enabling you. These hard things are not in our nature, which is why God works with and in us. Among and through us. Stronger together — and while one of us alone can't put the interests of others ahead of our personal interest, together we can.

And we are seeing the proof of that here. 13 students at breakfast on Wednesday. 27 kids in Music and Art. Leadership that has committed to making sure that outreach projects will continue. People who are willing to get up and be here at 6 am to fix breakfast. Willing to herd first and second graders who are carrying paint. Willing to tutor kids who need help. Willing to spend time — these things are hard.

Being of one mind, of one accord — this is hard amongst us here. When you put the entirety of Christ's Church into the mix, it's hard. We often fight more cruelly with other believers than we do with non-believers. But God, working in and among us, can help us get along with other believers, too.

This table, where we come to be fed and nurtured in the unity of Christ, is Christ's table. And this morning, on this World Communion Sunday, believers in every part of the world are coming to this table to be of one mind, one accord — one love.

To have the mind of Christ is to see what Christ sees. Our communion hymn this morning is *Be Thou My Vision* — and as we sing it, preparing to come to this one table that is set for the whole world, let us make it our prayer, that we would have one mind, one accord, one love.

Love Is All You Need
Romans 13.8-14; Matthew 18.15-20

As often happens, I think I know on Monday what the lectionary passages have to say, and then... things happen. Some weeks, there's so much the passages have to say there's no way to address them all – and as most of you well know, editing for brevity is not actually in my wheelhouse.

In the literal wake of two major hurricanes back to back – both setting records for rain totals, size, and in the case of Irma, plain old contentiousness – flooding in Nigeria; earthquake in Mexico; devastating fires in the northwest; serious health issues in our own church family and extended family....

With all that going on, it seems a bit precious to talk about loving one another, to talk about handling conflict among church members, to talk about living in the light. Instead, with all the disaster and uncertainty around us, it seems more prudent to talk instead about why God would allow such things to happen.

Some of us took the library trip up to Terre Haute yesterday to Candles Holocaust museum and heard Eva Kor[5] tell her story of survival and journey of forgiveness. The educational materials in the museum were overwhelming – it hardly seems real that so much evil was done by human beings to other human beings. And again, it seemed the prudent choice this morning is to talk about why God allows such things to happen.

Well, I don't know. I don't if God allows it, I don't know why things happen. God's ways are not our ways, and when we try to get our

---

[5] Eva Kor and her twin sister survived the medical experiments on twins at Auschwitz during WW II. She established a Holocaust museum in Terre Haute, IN, and works to encourage forgiveness, not as a matter of faith, but as something essential to retaining and reclaiming humanity.

head wrapped around the large-scale evil and disaster that is part and parcel of living in this world, we run the risk of trying to BE God – to explain it, reframe it, justify it, deny it. To let our own minds and imagination be judge and jury on what God will and will not allow, stand for, or condemn. To say that the landfall and resulting destruction of large areas and many people's lives is an act of retribution on the part of God is hubris. And hurtful. And certainly not helpful in furthering the good news of the coming kingdom.

Because whatever happens, as we heard God tell Moses from the burning bush: I am the one who is. And pretty much told Moses his questions were out of line. God is the one who is – and has cut us some marching orders that have nothing to do with trying to figure out what God does and does not allow, and who God does and does not hate. Because both passages this morning – in addition to some other things – say this: I love you. And you should love each other. And when you remember I love you and you go and love other people, then the evil is diffused, and the disasters are mitigated by help and companionship. Because we aren't to love people from afar. It's up close and personal.

Paul, in writing to the Roman church, was sending them his resume – working to convince them that he was indeed a true apostle of Jesus. So, it is not unintentional that he uses language that evokes Jesus: Love one another. And: the law is summed up by this: Love your neighbor. Jesus illustrated love your neighbor with a story about a Samaritan who helped a Jew in need. Hated enemy helping hated enemy. That's how you love your neighbor, according to Jesus. You get down in the ditch, get dirty, and use your time and money. Love, says Paul, evoking Jesus, is the fulfillment of the law.

Coupled with this, we have this passage from the gospel of Matthew, which is Jesus telling folks how to get along with each other in church. This passage is often used in church polity in a variety of situations, and quite frankly, has led to some awful things happening in churches. This method of handing problems in the church has covered up the evil of systemic child abuse, sexual abuse, harassment

– because Jesus seems to be telling us not to air our dirty laundry in public. And so, we don't. But we're perfectly happy to use this same passage to condemn others and keep our distance because we get to that sentence about treating the offender as a Gentile or a tax collector, and figure that we are off the hook. If someone continues to sin, it's a loophole in the "love your neighbor" thing.

Here's the thing, though: there is no loophole in that love your neighbor thing. It may seem like Jesus is telling us to shun these folks. But who did Jesus hang out with, talk to, eat with, defend? Gentiles and tax collectors. Indeed, Matthew – the writer of this gospel – was a tax collector in his other life.

So, if we're to treat continuing sinners as Gentiles and tax collectors, apparently, we're supposed to make them part of our inner circle. To love them.

When they hate you, love them. When they lie to you, love them. When they inconvenience you, love them. When they don't deserve it, love them. When they do terrible things to you, love them.

I think the most remarkable thing about Eva Kor yesterday was the peace in her face. For someone who had faced the worst evil humans can dream up, she has a remarkable calmness about her. And she alluded to the possibility it wasn't always that way. She said she had to decide to forgive the Nazis, and she did. In ways both public and private.

And she said something else I found worth repeating: she said very few people survived the camps who did not have a family member or close friend with them. Having someone else going into the horror kept alive the will to live. There are a few who survived alone – but, in her words, they lost their humanity to do it, and never regained it.

Jesus, in this passage from Matthew is warning us about this: we need each other. This is why we are to love one another, to resolve our conflicts and be able to reconcile with one another. Because we need one another. We need others to get down in the ditch with us, to bind us up, to remind us that each human being is created in the image of God – and to remind them of that.

There is much more to be said about this – and we don't have time to even scratch the surface, really. But I am struck by these words of Jesus: whatever you bind on earth will be bound in heaven, and whatever you loose on earth will be loosed in heaven.

If we keep our love bound up and close to us – loving from a distance (which frankly, I'm not sure is even possible), what does that mean in the life to come? Do we think the people we dislike, and fear will somehow be transformed in heaven? Or that we will be?

Jesus came to transform us here and now – to make us love others now. Not at some point in the future. Paul says time is running short, we are wasting daylight.

Love is the fulfilling of the law. And love requires us to do, not feel. Reconciliation with others is an act, not an emotion. Forgiveness is tangible, not an abstract idea.

During so much terror, destruction, uncertainty, and yes – downright un-neighborliness, it's sometime difficult that our mandate as Christians is to go forth in peace to love and serve. To be the good news of the gospel to others. Because when you boil it down, that's what teaching and preaching and making disciples is: being Jesus to other people.

So, we're out of time before we can get to the nuts and bolts of how that might work. But I would remind you that we, as a congregation, are doing many things that are works of love in the world. And it takes all of us: those that tutor, those that make meals, those that clean up, those that pray, those that write the checks.... And all those things help loose the love of Christ into the world. It's so much easier to keep it bound up, hold it close to protect it.

But that's the thing: love needs no protection. Love just needs people to DO it.

So, brothers and sisters, I remind you of the words of Paul: love one another. For the one that loves another has fulfilled the law. Go forth and be fulfillers of the law....

Pay Attention!
Exodus 3.1-5

I subscribe to this e mail commentary on the lectionary passages, and this week, the headline on the e mail was: Are you paying attention?

Which, frankly, got my attention.

Because, so much of the time, I – we – are not paying attention. We are floating through the days, wondering how we got from June to September, and never really paying the kind of attention that would let us truly see the world around us, and the people in it.

Moses was not paying attention. There had been some things happen between the story of the basket in the bulrushes and the herding sheep of today. Moses, raised as a member of Pharaoh's household, had been walking among the children of Israel one day and saw one of the slaves being beaten by an Egyptian overseer. Moses, who apparently had never **really** seen the enslavement of his people, even though he saw it every day, was enraged, and beat the Egyptian to death. Which, member of Pharaoh's house or not, meant trouble. So off Moses took, and found himself on the sheep farm of Jethro, married one of Jethro's daughters, and then found himself tending sheep in the middle of nowhere.

I'm pretty sure that occasionally, Moses asked himself, how did I get here? And since it was probably better to not pay too much attention to how different life could have been, I suspect his mind was wandering.

I think God would prefer that we pay attention. And when we don't, sometimes God will get our attention. I, myself, have been on the receiving end of God's theophany – which is the fancy seminary word for "appearance of God." I won't bore you with details, but it ended with me sitting in a chair, looking around and wondering what in the world had happened to the carefully constructed life I had.

And then a very unlikely source made an offhand reference to a burning bush – and suddenly I was paying attention.

Moses likely had a good life with his family in Midian, but there was work to do back in Egypt. And so God needed to get Moses' attention.

We need to be careful getting too comfortable with the way things are – it can cause us to lose sight of how things ought to be. It's easy to open our hearts and our wallets for those affected by hurricane Harvey – and we should. But relief agencies – and the Presbyterian Disaster Assistance is no exception – have made it so easy to give (text whatever to this number and give $20!) that it's easy to stop paying attention. We've helped. Now on to the next thing.

And the arm's length way of helping those in need can make it easier to ignore those closer to home also in need. And it can make it seem as if we are the primary actors in the playing out of God's work in our world. But, as we've seen in the story of Joseph, of the Hebrew midwives, and now of the grown Moses – the primary actor here is God. The one who is. The one who causes to be. The one who hears the cries of those who are oppressed.

The one who is always paying attention. And wants us to be paying attention, too. And when we lose focus, and stop seeing the world as God sees it, God will sometimes get our attention. But not only do we need to notice when God gets our attention – we need to make sure we have the message right.

The gospel passage from this week's' lectionary is from the gospel of Matthew, chapter 16, beginning in verse 21

> [21]*From that time on, Jesus began to show his disciples that he must go to Jerusalem and undergo great suffering at the hands of the elders and chief priests and scribes, and be killed, and on the third day be raised.* [22]*And Peter took him aside and began to rebuke him, saying, "God forbid it, Lord! This must never happen to you."* [23]*But he turned*

> and said to Peter, "Get behind me, Satan! You are a stumbling block to me; for you are setting your mind not on divine things but on human things."
>
> ²⁴Then Jesus told his disciples, "If any want to become my followers, let them deny themselves and take up their cross and follow me. ²⁵For those who want to save their life will lose it, and those who lose their life for my sake will find it. ²⁶For what will it profit them if they gain the whole world but forfeit their life? Or what will they give in return for their life? (NRSV)

How many times are we tempted to tell God what needs to be done? Who God is? Who God should be saving? Who God should listen to?

Just as Jesus told Peter – get behind me – God told Moses from that burning bush: Take off your shoes. You are in the presence of something so holy you can't even imagine. Now: pay attention.

Left to our own devices, we don't usually get it right. Moses was put in that basket and pulled out of the river so that he would be in the right place to lead God's people. But Moses wasn't paying attention – and so he ended up tending sheep. Peter, who had walked alongside Jesus from the beginning of his ministry, thought he knew what the Messiah was to be and do. He had not been paying attention.

Are we paying attention? Are we seeing the world as God sees the world, or are we seeing the world as we want God to see it? Do we hear the cries of the oppressed and hurting? Or do we hear a vague buzz in our ears, which we can drown out by texting to give?

It's easier to not pay attention, frankly. It saves time and energy to move about thinking we've got this, that we understand the problems perfectly, and have God on our side. But we need to remember: the story of God's work in the world is the story of God's will interacting with human agency. God will do what God will do – and it's always better if we get with that program rather than trying to dream up a new one and get God on board with that. You saw how that turned out for Peter. And all of Moses' very valid objections: they went nowhere.

This is the place where we learn to pay attention, the place where we are fed and nurtured and prepared to go out into the world to see it as God sees it. To hear and feel and do as God would do. This morning we have not a burning bush in front of us, but a table, lovingly prepared by a God who sees and hears – and pays attention. And asks us to do the same.

Faith Here and Now
Hebrews 11.1-16; Luke 12.32-40

Faith is one of those things that we think we know – we must know what it is. It's part of who we confess to be as Christians. We talk about faith in lots of ways. We talk about a community of faith. The Christian faith. Essentials of the faith. Faith of our fathers. Symbols of faith. Keep the faith. Blind faith. Crisis of faith. There are lots of quotes about faith – I have friends that have faith quotes as part of their e mail signature. Some of them are theologically good, some not so much.

I remember when I was a kid hearing my dad try to define faith. There was the chair example – you know, you can say that chair will hold you up, but it's not faith until you actually sit in it. Or the parachute – you can say it will keep you from slamming into the earth at 110 miles an hour, but you only have faith if you jump out of the airplane.

Faith is important to how we live our lives– my brother and his wife named their daughter Faith. It was a difficult pregnancy and they believed she would arrive healthy and beautiful. And she did. The whole family knows that it was their faith that played a huge part in that baby's safe arrival. My sister in law never doubted.

And remember those necklaces that had the little mustard seed in them? I had those – based on Matthew 17.20: if you have faith as small as a mustard seed, you can move mountains. My fear is that we often let Matthew 17.20 be our only definition of faith. That faith is some sort of divine ATM where the results we get are dependent on what we put into it. God is faithful and fulfills promises based on our amount of faith. If we are faithful, we can depend on God. If we are not faithful, we should not expect God to be there for us.

That's not faith – that's one hand scratching the other. The good news of the scripture is that God's faithfulness does not depend on us AT ALL. God keeps promises – even when we don't. And even when it seems impossible.

After the death and resurrection of Christ, the empire of Rome began to make things more difficult for Jews in Palestine. By the year 70, the temple in Jerusalem had been destroyed, and it was never rebuilt. Jews were often made to leave their homes, give up their property… And in the way that humans work because the Jews were oppressed by the Romans, they in turn were not so kind to Christians. During the early years of Christianity – Christians faced the most trouble from their own neighbors.

These first believers, who were Jews first, were often not allowed to attend synagogue. Not allowed to practice their faith by coming to the Temple to celebrate the holy days. The Hebrews – to whom this letter was written – suffered humiliation, separation from friends and family, loss of property, loss of the larger religious community. They may not have been threatened with facing the lions in the coliseum, but in some ways, this may have been worse.

It was becoming harder and harder to stand for what they believed during the humiliation, the separation, the losses. Some of them had stopped meeting for worship and the believer's meal. Their faith was not strong enough to withstand the thousand tiny cuts that being in constant opposition to "the ways things are" entailed.

Faith is more than simple belief. It's more than following a list of do's and don'ts. It's more than being able to recite a list of things we believe. The one thing that sets apart the people we read about in this chapter is this: their faith required two things – God to call and them to answer.

Professor of mine from seminary said this about faith – it is faith that allows us to know what cannot be truly known or proven. Just as God created the world out of nothing, so faith creates belief when there is no reason to believe – or when it's reasonable to believe. This is a gift from God – and it's not a gift that we can define in terms of one person, or even one community. This is a story that goes all the way back to Abraham and God's promise:

> **Genesis 15:5-7** *⁵ He brought him outside and said, "Look toward heaven and count the stars, if you are able to count them." Then he said to him, "So shall your descendants be." ⁶ And he believed the LORD; and the LORD ¹ reckoned it to him as righteousness. ⁷ Then he said to him, "I am the LORD who brought you from Ur of the Chaldeans, to give you this land to possess." (NRSV)*

Abraham never saw those descendants. Never possessed that land. Yet he knew God spoke the truth. How?

The answer is in verse 10: *For he looked forward to the city that has foundations, whose architect and builder is God.*

Faith that creates something out of nothing – belief when there is no reason to believe – this is faith that can see what is not yet here. We usually think of kingdom of God, as eternity as being in "the future" but they transcend time and space. They are eternal – both forward and backwards. Happening now, already happened, still to come – all at the same time. It's one of the mysteries of our faith.
When we share the Lord's Supper, during the Great Thanksgiving, we give thanks that we share the meal – "with believers in every time and place." Those who have come before, those who will come after. Eternity doesn't start at the end of this life and go on forever. It has already started – God's story is ongoing and never ending. It is only through the gift of faith that we can glimpse this and partially understand it.

But faith is not one dimensional – it is multi-faceted if I can mix metaphors here. Faith is not just the gift we received from God simply because God loves us. It is also our response to that gift. The trust, the gratitude we have in God – we respond to the gift of faith with our own faith in God. Faith that despite our own failings and faults, God remains faithful. Faith that despite whatever is going on in the world around us, the kingdom of God is near. Faith that however we are defined or described by our culture, our identity is "child of God."

If we have faith as a mustard seed, we might be able to move mountains – but why would we want to? But the ability to see the kingdom – now there's something worth having faith in, something that can keep us going in the dark days, survive the thousand ways the world tries to humiliate and define us. In the next chapter of Hebrews, chapter 12, the author says this:

> **Hebrews 12:1-2** NRS *Therefore, since we are surrounded by so great a cloud of witnesses, let us also lay aside every weight and the sin that clings so closely,[1] and let us run with perseverance the race that is set before us, 2 looking to Jesus the pioneer and perfecter of our faith, who for the sake of[1] the joy that was set before him endured the cross, disregarding its shame, and has taken his seat at the right hand of the throne of God.*

The result of our faith is getting free of the things that keep us from being faithful. Jesus showed us the way – faithful unto death. Faithful when we are not. Sets a table for us, invites us in, nurtures, feeds us during this great cloud of witnesses.

And for that, we respond in gratitude – thanks be to God.

Re-Focusing

Luke 10.38-42

So, I've made no secret of the fact that I hate housework. And if you don't know if you have serious dust allergies, I need notice before you come visit me.

But I also like to have company. And because I'm my mother's daughter, I can't have company unless my house is spotless and looks like no one lives there. This means that having company is stressful for me – and I don't want it to be. I've gotten better over the years about not obsessing about my clutter, or my dust, or the general disorder that tends to define my personal life. But still....

And over the years, I've heard this story of Martha and Mary used to criticize my tendency to over-think the correlation between the condition of my house and hospitality. Because when we hear this story, we tend to hear it as a criticism of the actual work Martha is doing, that we should always focus less on doing in our walk of discipleship and more on the listening part of discipleship.

But to take that interpretation of the story is to ignore everything else Jesus did. Jesus was big on the doing – the "go and do likewise" part of things. In fact, go and do likewise was the end of the parable we delved into last week – the story of the Good Samaritan.

And Jesus was equally big on the details of hospitality – in the story of the woman that anointed Jesus with the expensive oil, Jesus outlined for his host the places where the hospitality Jesus was offered was less than expected. Jesus himself set a high bar for hospitality. And in the upper room, Jesus himself took on the tasks of extreme hospitality as he washed the feet of his friends – even the friend he knew would betray him.

So, no, we shouldn't hear this story as pointing us away from either radical hospitality or the doing part of ministry. What we should hear, instead, is that whatever we're doing, what's most important is our focus.

Martha's mistake wasn't what she was doing – it was her focus while she was doing it.

If you have a sister, you probably have had this conversation with your mother: Mom, she's not doing as much as I am.

Far too often, we pay more attention to what other folks are doing than we do to our own efforts – and that applies to housework, yard work, work work – and especially disciple work. And I think we do that – at least I do – to make sure that I'm not expending any more effort than necessary. It seems ridiculous to say it out loud, but I suspect a great many people spend more time making sure they are not overdoing it on the Christian discipleship thing than they would just giving up and really, really asking what Jesus would do.

And that's where we get off track like Martha. We have an easier time of it, though, because Jesus isn't sitting in our living rooms to take us to task when we complain that sometimes being a disciple of Christ is just too hard. And, frankly, no one else is working at it quite as hard as we are…

But like Martha, the problem is not the work, or the amount or difficulty of it, but our focus – which tends to be on ourselves.

Matthew 11:30: Jesus tells us that when we follow him, the yoke is easy, and the burden is light. But we don't often feel that way. We feel constrained by the commands of Jesus to love one another, to live in unity, to bear one another's burdens – it's **hard** to do all that. There are people who don't love us back. There are people who aren't deserving of our love, much less our actual help. Like Martha, our focus is off.

I want to be clear – hospitality IS important. Making others welcome, making sure they are fed and cared for – this is important work, and work that is vital to the kingdom of God. God welcomes us, nurtures us, feeds us, cares for us – and we are to do that for others.

Martha's focus should have been on the **why** – not the what. Why do we welcome others? Feed others? Love others? Not for our own well-being and warm fuzziness, even though that might be a by-product. But that's not WHY we do it.

We do it, so the world can see Jesus in us – we do it because God does these things for us, and our only way of showing our thanks is to do it for others.

The gospel of Luke is full of stories, parables, metaphors – part of why I like it so much. Matthew's gospel is much more down to earth, practical. Jesus wasn't being completely metaphorical in Matthew when he said the yoke is easy, the burden light.

When we are following Jesus with the proper focus – on Jesus, not ourselves or other people – the burden IS light. Mary, in sitting at the feet of the Master, was likely bathed in joy. Martha, focused on her own efforts and the lack of gratitude she perceived – not only from the rest of the family but from Jesus himself – was bathed in resentment. Mary's burden – light. Martha's – no so much.

Jesus was not telling Martha that her sister had chosen the better part because she wasn't engaged in the hospitality work – work Jesus proved over and over he valued highly. But because Mary was focused on Jesus – that was the better choice.

It really is a matter of focus…. And I fear that our focus is less on our own nearness to Jesus and more on sizing up other's nearness to Jesus. We have an awful lot of people in the world who want to be the deciders on who is and isn't in the righteousness club – who, like Martha, want to point out where others are not holding up their end of the yoke, making our burden difficult. People who aren't good Christians like us…. But I digress. This is about where our focus should be, not where it shouldn't be….

Elsewhere in the gospel of Matthew, Jesus says this to his followers:

> *31 When the Son of Man comes in his glory, and all the angels with him, then he will sit on the throne of his glory. 32 All the nations will be gathered before him, and he will separate people one from another as a shepherd separates the sheep from the goats, 33 and he will put the sheep at his right hand and the goats at the left. 34 Then the king will say to those at his right hand, "Come, you that are blessed by my Father, inherit the kingdom prepared for you from the foundation of the world; 35 for I was hungry and you gave me food, I was thirsty and you gave me something to drink, I was a stranger and you welcomed me, 36 I was naked and you gave me clothing, I was sick and you took care of me, I was in prison and you visited me." 37 Then the righteous will answer him, "Lord, when was it that we saw you hungry and gave you food, or thirsty and gave you something to drink? 38 And when was it that we saw you a stranger and welcomed you, or naked and gave you clothing? 39 And when was it that we saw you sick or in prison and visited you?" 40 And the king will answer them, "Truly I tell you, just as you did it to one of the least of these who are members of my family, you did it to me." 41 Then he will say to those at his left hand, "You that are accursed, depart from me into the eternal fire prepared for the devil and his angels; 42 for I was hungry and you gave me no food, I was thirsty and you gave me nothing to drink, 43 I was a stranger and you did not welcome me, naked and you did not give me clothing, sick and in prison and you did not visit me." 44 Then they also will answer, "Lord, when was it that we saw you hungry or thirsty or a stranger or naked or sick or in prison, and did not take care of you?" 45 Then he will answer them, "Truly I tell you, just as you did not do it to one of the least of these, you did not do it to me." 46 And these will go away into eternal punishment, but the righteous into eternal life.' (NRSV)*

When we are focused on things other than Jesus, we run the risk of missing an opportunity to do the things Jesus expects – to feed, to clothe, to visit, to love. We miss seeing the least of these.

I believe the difference between the sheep and the goats is less about our own sense of righteousness, and more about focus.
Where is our focus? Is it on making sure that everything and everyone is doing right? Are we focused on the preparations for Jesus' return to the detriment of the people who are around us every day? Are we busy, yet accomplishing nothing of what God would have us do? Are we followers of Jesus, focused on doing the things he told us, or are we holding ourselves and others to human standards of behavior?

Where is our focus this morning, as we prepare to go out of this sanctuary and out into a world that is very clear that it would like our focus to NOT be on loving others as we are loved. Not focused on thankful living. Not focused on the living Word of God who came to us to show and tell us of God's love for us and others.

Are we Mary? Bathed in joy? Or are we Martha? Covered in resentment? Christ centered? Or self-centered?

I'm not saying it's easy – people don't come much more self-absorbed than me. And loving others is hard – and dangerous. But it's what we've got.

Come to me – my yoke is easy, my burden light. I read an article this week that said if the yoke isn't easy, and the burden isn't light – we're not doing it right. We're not properly focused.

So – in the ongoing effort to make things easier on myself, I'm going to see if I can't change my focus a bit, get a bit closer to Jesus. I wear glasses, so I know what a difference a slight change in focus can make – and I'm hoping that this week, a slight change in focus will change what I see. That I will see more of the least of these, that I will see ways I can be more loving of those that aren't exactly loveable. Change my focus from my work, my rewards, my feelings – and focus instead on the mandate of Christ to love others as I am loved.

Kum Bah Ya

Ephesians 4.25-5.2; John 6.35,41-51

My favorite comic strip is *Pearls Before Swine*. It's a bit irreverent, a lot funny, and says quite a bit about how we get along with each other. There is Pig, who is the innocent, gullible childlike character who sees good in everyone. Then there's Rat, who is jaded, cynical, and sees good in nothing. Then there is Zebra, who is hunted by his neighbors the crocodiles, who luckily are the world's worst hunters. Anyway, the comic strip is about how all these animals live together.

The crocs try to lure the zebra into various funny traps, so they can eat them, Rat is always trying to put one over on Pig, and occasionally they all go visit the comic artist who draws them, so they can complain about how things are going. There's one where all the characters were holding hands, singing *Kum Bah Ya*. When the comic artist asked what they were doing, they told him they were raising money to save newspapers. The artist kind of scoffed at that, and said, hey, newspapers aren't going anywhere. But if you're wrong, said Rat, and newspapers become a thing of the past, then you'll have to go back to being a lawyer. In the last panel, the artist has joined hands with all the characters and is singing *Kum Bah Ya, My Lord*....

When we start talking about how Christians ought to live together, there's a parallel here. Sometimes, we're in denial about the whole situation, and don't want to look at things clearly. Or we are so quick to write off the idea of church that there's nothing to do but join hands and sing *Kum Bah Ya*. Even before the church really started, we see in the gospel passage there were problems. Jesus speaks, and immediately the religious leaders begin to try and find a way for it to mean something less troublesome. No *Kum Bah Ya* there....

In his letter to the church at Ephesus Paul intends to tell us how we should live together as Christ's church. This letter was written late in the first century – after Christians had a bit of experience about being

Church together. Apparently, they were finding themselves fighting amongst each other, treating each other badly – no *Kum Bah Ya* there.

This is written to the church by a man who knows he doesn't have long to live. He's in prison, he's old, and this is the last letter he'll likely have time to write. So, this is chock full of good advice about what's really important when it comes to being the Church of Christ. Some scholars think that Ephesians was not written just for the Church at Ephesus but was intended to be circulated around to all the churches in Asia Minor, with a fill in the blank for the church name. There's very little personal information in the letter, which is unusual for Paul. This advice is meant to be more widespread than Paul's usual communication.

Prior to this passage Paul spent three chapters reminding us of the magnitude of God's love for us, about the lavish riches of God's grace. God's love is not measured out in teaspoons, but rather comes flooding down upon us in lavish excess. At chapter 4, however, we move from the "what" of God's love to the "So What?"
So, what? So, what if God loves us, loves creation, loves everyone and everything in the world with a lavishness that we can't comprehend. What does that mean? So, what comes next?

At the beginning of this chapter, Paul tells us we are to live a life worthy of our calling. Live a life worthy of the lavish waters of baptism that are poured out upon us. A life claimed by God. A life fed by the bread of life. This morning, Paul begins to talk about how that happens.

And this is where it gets dangerous. It's always great to talk about God's love and the transforming power of grace. Where it sometimes gets sticky is when we talk about what that transformation should look like. These verses in the fourth chapter of Ephesians are, at first glance, a laundry list of does and don'ts for behavior. Don't sin. Don't be angry. Don't steal. Work hard. Talk nicely. Be kind. Live in love.

And we love such a list, especially when it comes to the behavior of someone else. If we catch our kids in a lie, we pull out verse 25 – speak the truth to one another. When someone treats us badly – verse 32: be kind. When someone acts badly, verse 32 again: be imitators of Christ. But we need to put this passage into the context of the entire letter – Paul is not just telling the church members how to act so they can get along and feel good about each other. Paul is telling the church how to live up to the calling of Christ through baptism that joins us into the Church that is to accomplish God's will on earth. God has a plan – a plan to reconcile the world, which includes humanity – and the church is the means. This has implications way beyond our ability to get along. This is where we join Paul this morning. Then – as now – good church folk have a way of letting their own behavior get in the way of God's plans.

This laundry list that Paul give us this morning, is not just a list of things to do (or don't do) for the sake of not doing them. There are reasons, and not always the reasons we attach.

Thieves are to stop stealing – not because personal property is to be preserved, but because they can then engage in honest work IN ORDER TO SHARE IT WITH THOSE WHO HAVE LESS, those who might need to steal to live.

We are to speak no evil, not because we might hurt someone's feelings, but so we might give grace to someone. We are to forgive each other and be kind to each other, not so we can get along but because we are to be like Christ. Everything Paul says not to do is replaced with something we SHOULD do. And all these things we should do are to be done for one reason: the building up of the community of faith. Not the personal good of any one person, but for the building up of the unit of which we are all members.

Stealing is wrong. Being unkind is wrong. Being unwilling to forgive is wrong. But Paul goes beyond the simple right and wrong of these actions and into the why. These things hurt the family of God because they get in the way of God's ultimate plan of redemption, of reconciliation. And we aren't just to stop these bad behaviors, we are to replace them with different behaviors that DO work toward God's ultimate plan of redemption.

Don't just stop stealing. Stop stealing and then give to others. By the way, this assumes that those of us who are not forced to steal to live are already giving to others, but that's another sermon.

Don't speak evil, but rather be kind, lift others. Put some grace into the life of others. And Paul doesn't say don't be angry – what Paul says is be angry, but don't let it lead you into sin. Be angry – but you still must be kind. Be angry – but you still must add grace to the lives of others. Be angry, but you still must forgive. There is plenty in this world to be angry about – just as there was plenty in the world of Paul to be angry about. He was in prison, about to be executed, for goodness sake. But despite the anger, Paul remained concerned about reconciliation. About the life of Christians together. About the WHY of how we should be, over and above the HOW we should be.

Frankly, Paul gets in all the HOW we should be with a pun. Yep, a pun.

In verse 32, when you read it in the Greek, the word kind is *christoi*, which sounds like Christos, the word for Christ. We are to be *christoi*, like Christos. We are to be Christ for other people.

Ok, I see you nodding along with that one. Be kind. Check. Not steal, but give to others, check. No evil, slander, malicious talk. Check. We are, we are like Christ. We are *christoi*, like Christos.

Yeah…. but see, Paul goes on and this is not in short hand, even though we skip over it a lot. We are to be Christ for others, as Christ is for us. And Christ died for us. The assurance of pardon says it all: Christ died for us, rose for us, reigns in power for us, prays for us. Everything Christ is and was gets put on the line for others. Christ is the bread of life – feeding and nurturing a world that hasn't earned it, doesn't deserve it, and will likely resent it. And this is what Paul is saying to us this morning, just as he was telling the churches in Asia Minor just before his own execution. It's not about you – it's about us, the community of faith, and God's plan for the world.

And here we get down to the heart of Paul's message this morning: this list of don'ts isn't designed for the people "out there." It's given directly to the church people. Those outside the walls – we don't get to pull this list out and compare their behavior to this framework. It's not for them. We don't get to have ANY expectations about how they are to behave – they aren't part of the community of faith where we are. Paul wasn't talking to them. He was talking to us.

What would happen if instead of expecting other people to act like Christ, we starting acting Christ-like ourselves? Instead of worrying how people out there treat us, we begin being kind to the people we think are the unkindest. If instead of trying to convince the thieves out there to stop stealing, we instead started giving what we have to the thieves, so they wouldn't have to steal it? And we do it, not to change their behavior, or to heap those coals of fire on their head, but rather to CHANGE US. Rather than wait for people to change before we change the way we see them, we change how we see them with absolutely no expectation they will change?

There's nothing in this passage about how people outside the church ought to act. It's all about us – how WE should be, should act, should treat people. And the ONLY goal is this: to build up our own community of faith. To edify us. To transform us. Not others. US. We're the ones who need the transformation.

Ugh. That's not as pleasant a message. But it's real. Be imitators of Christ, Paul says. Give up yourselves, get over yourselves, and become an offering and sacrifice for others. Be christoi as Christos.

Sowing and Reaping–An Exercise in Hope

Galatians 6: 7-10

Every year about this time, I engage in some strange behavior. I order seed and flower catalogs. I prowl around the garden department at Home Depot and Lowes. I read packages of potting soil. I look at landscape timbers – looking for just the right length and making sure they are straight. I pick up and put down every flower on every shelf – looking for the perfect flat of pansies. I analyze the differences between Big Boy and roma tomatoes. I stand on the porch, survey the property, and envision a massive landscaping project, complete with koi pond and graveled path. When spring comes, the farming gene that runs in my family begins its dominate phase.

This creates a problem – because when it comes to me, the farming gene apparently got mutated somewhat. I love seed catalogs. I love to pick fresh tomatoes – to go to the strawberry fields and pick fresh berries. I love flower beds. But when the time comes to actually PLANT any of those things, that's where I fall short.

I have gone so far as to order dozens of plants from catalogs. Buy several flats of flowers and vegetables from the garden shop. And plant NONE of it. I have the greatest of longings for a garden, and all the best intentions. But the reality is, I also have non-existent gardens. There are things growing in the space I gaze at longingly, but not things I've planted, and it's certainly not the garden of my dreams.

I have learned to adapt – over the years I found some plants that I could plant one time, require little maintenance and I'm able to have at least the semblance of growing things, and I've learned to grow in pots on the porch, but gardening in general is not something for which I have great follow up skills. The desire is there – the follow up non-existent.

The reality is that no matter how many seed catalogs I order, no matter how many trips I take to Home Depot, no matter how much I long to look out the kitchen window and see beautiful rows of tomato plants, none of those things will get me a beautiful garden. I have to go outside and get my hands a bit dirty. If I want tomatoes, I have to actually plant the tomatoes.

For the Galatians, this was not the problem. The church was planted and apparently growing just fine, thank you. But they had been visited by some very helpful missionaries who were telling them things weren't quite right. There were some things missing from their gardens, apparently.

The missionaries agreed with Paul that salvation came from grace alone, but that wasn't all. There were things you were supposed to do. Rules you were supposed to follow. And if you didn't do those things or follow those rules, well… it might be that the grace of your salvation might be in question.

To which Paul says – Nonsense. You Galatians have been freed from the list of shalt's and shalt not's. And more to the point, you're wasting time. There is much to be done, and time is finite. We can't afford the luxury of worrying about things like this.

You shall sow what you reap.

You know I think most of us have heard this passage so many times that we tune it out. What you sow, you will reap. It's a warning, right? Well, yes it is, at least it was when my mother said it. It's a warning much like my other favorite of Mom's: you made your bed young lady and now you must lie in it. But I digress.

This is a warning, BUT there is also a promise here – If we sow peace, we will have peace. If we sow love, we will be loved. What we plant – that determines our harvest.

It's important that we be aware of what we plant. Because we are planting all the time, whether we realize it or not. Unlike me and my unplanted pansies, in the garden of life we are always planting. And if we're not intentional about what we plant, we might not like the harvest. We are either sowing to harvest a crop of the flesh, or a crop of the Spirit. The Galatians, Paul warns, are on the brink of sowing a crop that deals with mortal things, things that are tinged with the death that will come to all things. Things that cannot and will not last.

What they – and we – should be sowing is a crop of the Spirit. This harvest will be of lasting things. Things that matter. Things that should not be confused with unimportant things. In fact, I believe Paul would argue that it is the harvest of the Spirit that makes this life valuable, important and pleasing to God.

Sowing to the flesh – to this world, the mortal world – is to spend time and energy worrying about things that don't improve our relationship to others or to God.

At the end of chapter 5, Paul lays out the differences between what is harvested from the flesh as opposed to what is harvested from the Spirit. In chapter 5, verses 19 through 23, Paul says this:

> *Now the works of the flesh are obvious: fornication, impurity, licentiousness, idolatry, sorcery, enmities, strife, jealousy, anger, quarrels, dissensions, factions, envy, drunkenness, carousing, and things like these. I am warning you, as I warned you before: those who do such things will not inherit the kingdom of God. By contrast, the fruit of the Spirit is love, joy, peace, patience, kindness, generosity, faithfulness, gentleness, and self-control.*

If you put these two lists up against one another, the fundamental difference between the fruits of the flesh and fruits of the Spirit is the self-indulgence involved. Paul says that when we sow to the flesh, we sow to our OWN flesh – it's all about us. Our being right. Our being happy. Our being self-fulfilled. Our feeling satisfied. Our feeling okay. The harvest of the flesh comes back to us. And none of this harvest of the flesh will outlast our mortal life.

On the other hand, the fruits of the Spirit are not about us. Love, peace, patience, kindness – these are NOT self-indulgent and are totally about others. We cannot sow to our own spirit, but only to THE Spirit. And these fruits will outlast our time here, spreading and taking over.

My questionable gardening skills has at least given me a limited understanding and appreciation for plants and their life cycles. There are two kinds of flowers – annuals and perennials. Annuals tend to be more showy, more spectacular, but they have to be replanted year after year. They have one season. One of my favorite annuals is a hybrid petunia – the wave petunia. You've probably seen them – the flowers tend to be smaller, but they spread like ivy. They're incredibly easy to grow. They're great for hanging baskets. But if you plant them in a bed, over the course of a summer, one decent plant can cover a square yard of ground. And as long as you keep pulling off the dead blooms – deadheading – they will bloom and bloom and bloom all summer long.

But once it gets cold, petunias don't look all that good. One good frost, one really cold night and they are gone, never to be revived. That square yard of ground goes from being a riot of spectacular color to covered with brown, spindly, ugly carcasses of petunias.
Daisies, on the other hand, not so showy. They spread, but very slowly. And they bloom, and the blooms stay for a while, but then they're done for the season. Very low maintenance. Some people would even think boring. But here's the thing – they come up, year after year. When they stop blooming, the green foliage is still there, with the promise of new life next spring. That foliage is there in the

garden with the promise of things to come and I know there will be flowers in my garden next summer even if I can't see them now.
There is a season for planting, the wise sage in Ecclesiastes tell us. We can plant too early, but in my case, I often wait much too late. And when you go to the garden store late, you don't always get the best choices of plants. I often pass those by – why would I want to spend my time planting something that won't live and produce?

We only have so much time, says Paul to the Galatians. And to us. Why would we want to spend the time we have sowing and planting things that won't last? Or by allowing unwanted plants to come into our garden space? What we sow, we WILL reap – even the stuff we sow unknowingly. This is the blessing and the curse.

Time is limited – Paul wants the Galatians to use it to build up the family of faith, the community garden, not to tear it down by arguing.

We will reap, says Paul. And we will reap what is sown, whether we take the time and effort to sow it or simply leave it to chance.
This is too important to leave to chance. We must make sure we are sowing what we seek to harvest.

We can't reap a harvest of love and peace by spending our time dwelling on who's right and who's wrong any more than I can have a lovely garden by paging through seed and plant catalogs. At the end the day – at the end of our days – the garden plot of our lives will either have the browned remains of our self-indulgence or the foliage of things to come, awaiting the re-emergence of blooms over and over.

Let us then, in the time that we have, be sure that we are working to fill our gardens with the things that will give us love, joy, peace, patience, kindness, generosity, faithfulness, gentleness, and self-control. Let us work for the good of all.

www.ingramcontent.com/pod-product-compliance
Lightning Source LLC
Chambersburg PA
CBHW052144110526
44591CB00012B/1851